Secrets

Secrets

LINNY STOVALL, EDITOR

A LEFT BANK BOOK

BLUE HERON PUBLISHING, INC.
HILLSBORO, OREGON

Secrets

A Left Bank Book

Copyright © 1996 by Blue Heron Publishing, Inc.

Left Bank Books is an imprint of Blue Heron Publishing, Inc. All rights reserved.

ISBN 0-936085-33-9

Editor: Linny Stovall

Editorial Assistants: Elizabeth Jackson, Ingrid Opsahl, Peter Sears, Jessica Shulsinger

Cover and interior design: Dennis Stovall

Cover photographs: Cherie Hiser

Advisors: Ann Chandonnet, Madeline DeFrees, David James Duncan, Katherine Dunn, Jim Hepworth, Ursula K. Le Guin, Lynda Sexson, J.T. Stewart, Alan Twigg, Shawn Wong.

Left Bank Books are thematic collections. *Secrets* is the ninth title in the series.

"A Question of Class" by Dorothy Allison from *Skin, Talking About Sex, Class & Literature* is reprinted by permission of Firebrand Books, Ithaca, New York. Copyright © 1994 by Dorothy Allison.

Hobo graphics courtesy of *Symbols, Signs & Signets*, Ernst Lehner, Dover Publications, Inc., New York.

First edition, January 1996

Printed in the United States of America on pH-balanced paper.

Contents

Introduction: Postwar Secrets

Elinor Langer

1

One day when I was fifteen, I was sitting in the car outside my house waiting for my mother to drive me to the beach when, puzzled at the delay, I walked back in, picked up the telephone receiver, which was sitting on a table in the downstairs hallway, and heard my mother speaking on the upstairs extension in her bedroom saying in a quiet voice: "You really love her, don't you?" It was at that instant that I learned the importance of secrets. The words explained so much. Why for almost ten years an assistant to my father at the clothing store he had managed in western Massachusetts who was the same age as my older sister had been mentioned so much at the dinner table it was almost as if she were a member of the family. Why unlike me and my sister she was evidently incapable of doing any wrong. Why he begrudged my sister money to go to a private college when poor Sheila Robb had to work for a living and yet was so eager to learn. Why only two nights before when my father was complaining at dinner as usual that he couldn't get competent help in the downtown Boston store he managed now and I said "Why don't you hire Sheila Robb?" my mother had stopped eating with her food halfway to her mouth and gazed at him with an expression I had never observed before. Why the next night when we had gone out to dinner in the middle of the week, which also never happened, the evening had been unaccountably strange. Never mind what it did to my heart, which is a longer story, but the news of my father's affair shattered my impressionable adolescent brain into two intellectual hemispheres labeled "Appearance" and "Reality" and the knowledge that something unseen can have so much power dominated my life for a long time to come. It even determined my choice of work. As an investigative reporter in Washington, D.C., in the early 1960s I specialized in exposing things the government did not want known, such as the classified research program in chemical and biological weapons, where the gap between America's idealistic pretensions and its immoral practices would be particularly glaringly revealed. Gradually I came to find that distinction too simple and I moved on to other writing where neither "Appearance" nor "Reality" could be quite so readily described. But I still think they go a long way.

2

The hollow marriage was not my family's only secret: there was also the secret of being Jews, not "secret" exactly, but best not made too much of in those times lest it lead to that thing that everyone knew and did not know was happening in Germany, whose outlines were as yet only dimly understood. The Nazi extermination program was the biggest single secret of the war era, affecting not only the life of every Jew, but of every German, past, present, and future, and perhaps of all humanity. Our entire understanding of the moral nature of human beings was changed by it. The efforts of the Holocaust revisionists to deny it now are only a tribute to its power. A second enormous secret was the atomic bomb which similarly changed our understanding not only of our technological but of our theological condition, making "Man" a potential agent of destruction on a scale previously reserved to the gods. "The physicists have known sin," said Manhattan Project director J. Robert Oppenheimer, and while they and the rest of the world have had a respite, there has been no redemption. A third secret was the collapse of even the most rudimentary protections for citizens in the Soviet Union and the devolution of the state into a system of interlocking gulags that eventually swallowed up 19 million people, a system so powerful that even those literally staring it in the face, such as United States Vice-President Henry Wallace on his wartime visit to Kolyma, could not see what they were seeing, and when in the town of Kolpashevo on the river Ob in western Siberia an early thaw one spring revealed more than a thousand corpses still recognizable by the people alive at the time, they quickly covered them up again because they did not know what else to do.[†] Glancing over my books in preparation for these notes I see that the entire history of American postwar foreign policy could be written as a chronology of secrets: the overthrows, assassinations, and attempted assassinations of Muhammed Mussadegh in Iran (1953), of Jacobo Arbenz in Guatemala (1954), of Patrice Lumumba in the Congo (1961), of Fidel Castro in Cuba (1961–), of Salvador Allende in Chile (1973), and almost the whole of the Vietnam war beginning at least with the coup against Ngo Dinh Diem (1963) but particularly the clandestine operations against the North that culminated in the Gulf of Tonkin Resolution (1964) — and these events are only the most well known. Domestically, too, look what has happened in the dark: the persecution of Martin Luther King (1963–), the murder of Black Panther Fred Hampton (1969), and the subversion and intimidation of all the protest and resistance movements throughout the 1960s by the dirty tricksters of the FBI and the CIA of which these two cases can stand for the period as a whole; the affairs of the President of the United States with, among others, the mistress of a soon-to-be-murdered Mafia don involved in the Castro assassination plots (1961), the ex-wife of a CIA official, herself killed in an unsolved attack while strolling along Washington's peaceful C&O canal (1962), and — along with his brother, the Attorney General — Marilyn Monroe (1962); and the numerous 'gates, beginning with Watergate (1972) of which I hereby offer my own favorite, Hoovergate: the posthumous revelation not only of J. Edgar's semi-repressed homosexuality, which partly accounts for his use of it as a tool of torment against others, but also of his appearance in drag at a party given by Roy Cohn at the Plaza wearing "a fluffy black dress, very fluffy, with flounces, and lace stockings, and high heels and a black curly wig. He had makeup on, and false eyelashes. It was a very short skirt, and he was sitting there in the living room of the suite with his legs crossed."[††] At a subsequent party of Cohn's he was wearing a feather boa. Now, twenty years after the House and Senate intelligence investigations revealed many of these secrets and more and tried to institute reform, we learn that for the past ten years, under three different leaders, the CIA has deliberately given the White House and the Pentagon false information on which they have based decisions costing billions of dollars in order to protect its double agents in Moscow, a bureaucratic implosion in which the secrets of the agency have come to seem more important than the secrets of the world, which is perhaps just as well because it tells us better than anything else that we have truly come to the end of the postwar era. There were secrets in American political life long before World War II became the Cold War. But they were never so many, nor so heavy.

3

My deepest involvement with other people's secrets came during my decade writing the biography of the American radical writer Josephine Herbst. Josie had three important secrets. In 1920, in New York, she had an abortion, an episode forever linked in her mind with the death in Sioux City, Iowa, of her youngest sister, Helen, also from an abortion, around the same time. In 1932, she fell passionately in love with a woman painter whom she met at the artists' colony Yaddo, a passion which brought about the end of her marriage. And in the mid-Depression winter of 1934–35, at the apartment of her husband in Washington, D.C., she met a grandly conspiratorial character from the Communist Party underground who called himself "Carl," meetings that made her a witness not only to the existence of a clandestine cell of government employees known as the "Ware group" who were also members of the Communist Party, but to the truth of some of "Carl's" — Whittaker Chambers — later accusations against Alger Hiss. What fascinated me as her biographer was the inverse relationship between the centrality of these secrets in her life and their marginality in her papers. Josephine Herbst was an inexhaustible chronicler of her own existence and for most of the significant events in her life there were a seemingly endless number of sources. For her friendship with Ernest Hemingway, for example, there were a long, unpublished manuscript about Key West, an unpublished memoir of her childhood and youth, an uncompleted novella in which Hemingway is the central character, a memoir of the Spanish Civil War in which he plays an important role, a great number of miscellaneous notes and jottings including a journal kept in Spain, and a substantial correspondence not only with one of Hemingway's major biographers but with a number of other scholars, editors, and participants in the events she describes — and this is a case in which the communications between the principals themselves were relatively sparse. Her accounts of her mother's death, to take an example of a different kind, could be found in letters written to friends at the time it happened, in two of her novels, in notes for her memoirs, and in the memoirs themselves. With the secrets, however, this characteristic abundance did not exist. It was hard to find out what happened. Her abortion was hinted at only in a set of letters between the sisters that ended with Helen's death and in an unpublished autobiographical novel. Her affair was documented only in the letters between the women themselves and in some of her final exchanges with her husband. Her knowledge of the Communist underground in Washington left hardly any traces at all. Nor did she talk about them much. Josephine Herbst was as famous a talker as she was a writer and in her later years some of the finest writers in America gathered at her Pennsylvania farmhouse to hear her stories, but they never heard these. The things that meant the most to her she kept to herself. Gradually as I began to understand the relationship between silence and importance in Josie I began to understand it elsewhere as well. Silences speak. An affair...a child in trouble...a looming diagnosis...these circumstances of life which explain so much of the past and control so much of the future: How often are they mentioned only at the end of dinner when the check has already been ordered and the dishes have already been cleared, even between very good friends? Why do people have secrets? Like unhappy families, the reasons are probably always unique, but, to attempt generalization: to protect themselves not from the secret as such, which they themselves obviously know, and not even necessarily from the world, which in many cases will know it soon enough, but from having to deal with someone else's intrusions into matters that for whatever reasons are too painfully close to the heart. My mother's fatal cancer was like that. "Gall bladder," she told everyone after its discovery until the deception could no longer be sustained, and when I asked her why, she said "I don't want people to know I'm on the way out," meaning not only "I don't want to *be* on the way out, dammit, I don't want to die!" but "I can deal with this better on my own." Why do you have secrets? When I asked my almost ten-year-old son who is just getting the hang of them why children have secrets, he replied — immediately — "None of your business."

4

"Personal" and "political" hardly exhaust the categories of secrets. There are secrets of the confessional, secrets of the police precinct, secrets of the marketplace, secrets of the couch. Nor are the categories necessarily exclusive. "I've found it, but if I shout 'Eureka!' Billsely over there will know I've found it," reads a *New Yorker* cartoon of a suspicious scientist from a few years back and whether his secret is professional or personal would be hard to decide. Whatever its origin, any secret becomes a personal secret simply by the fact that it is held. But "personal" and "political" secrets seem particularly naturally to overlap. If you had known, in the 1950s, that the middle-aged man who was the director of your community theater and your daughter's drama coach was a blacklisted Hollywood screenwriter working under a false name, and you didn't tell, would the secret have been "personal" or "political"? Or — I'm not saying this happened — suppose in the 1970s you had a dear friend who had had to go underground and you received a phone call one day saying if you wanted to see her she would be in Golden Gate Park at a certain time and you went to Golden Gate Park and you saw your friend and she slipped away again, and you didn't tell, is that "personal" or "political" or both? The friendship is personal but does it become political because from then on you are keeping a political secret? What would it be if you were followed, and the San Francisco Red Squad next came after you? Where power is involved a personal secret can have vast political consequences. To return to J. Edgar Hoover: if you have a secret it is logical enough to assume that others do too. Is it too fanciful to imagine that if Hoover had been straight — or gayness accepted — the whole paranoid course of American domestic politics from 1924 when he became Director of the FBI to 1972 when he died, which has left such a dark legacy, might have been averted?

5

The only way to explore the complicated human territory into which the question of secrets immediately draws us is through art. It is only art that can unite the experiences of the wife and the mistress, the Jew and the Nazi, the radical and the FBI agent, the guilty physicist and the innocent victim, into a single story. At the 80th birthday celebration for Arthur Miller in New York, playwright John Guare revealed that it had taken the film of *Death of a Salesman*, which he had seen with his father at age 12, to dislodge the secret that his father told no one else in the family: that he himself had once been a salesman in Los Angeles and "It hadn't worked out." If you want to understand what is really happening — Appearance and Reality — between the same covers, you need literature. Here are some SECRETS to begin with. Pass it on.

---

† Adam Hochschild, *The Unquiet Ghost, Russians Remember Stalin*, Viking, 1994.
†† Anthony Summers, *The Secret Life of J. Edgar Hoover*, Pocket Star Books, 1994, p. 292-293.

The Confusion of Learning

Hollis Giammatteo

My parents had a friendship of sorts with the Gillespis. It was because of Christian Science. Cy was the organist at the church, and Gerri the first reader, and Bunny was their daughter my age. There are no ministers in Christian Science, just official readers of the weekly lessons. Until we turned twenty-one, us kids stayed in the basement for Sunday School. Bunny and I went together and sat at small, round tables in a bright room and were taught the principles by Mrs. Gangwhar. The building was new and the walls were smooth and white. On the wide molding were painted in golden script the synonyms for God: Truth, Beauty, Life, Love, Mind, Principle, and Soul. They circled the clean periphery like dancing maidens.

We weren't best friends or anything. She was called "slow," although she hadn't always been so. When we were little, I remember she loved to twirl in her dresses, or roll down their back yard hill if in dungarees, and we laughed lots. The school where she went now was special — Swaine Country Day School. It took kids with problems, and she'd gone for the last five years.

Bunny was still cute, though, with red hair like her mother's, and chocolate brown eyes like her dad's. Her freckles looked as if someone had dusted her lightly with cinnamon. But her eyes sometimes flattened and got hard, and then I remembered telephone conversations between my mother and Gerri Gillespi where I heard "Oh, I'm so sorry" interspersed with "What kind of spells?" and talk about the experts. The problem was, as Christian Scientists, we weren't allowed to be sick. It was considered an evil that had slipped into a person's mind to weaken it, and then a practitioner was called in to pray and return right thinking.

Once Bunny had a spell in Sunday School. She got very quiet, hunched over her fingers, beginning to pick and chew. Mrs. Gangwhar looked at Bunny from her light blue, loving eyes and slid her chair closer. She pulled Bunny's hands apart and held them and said, "Bunny, dear, tell me what you're thinking." Bunny stared back at Mrs. Gangwhar as if she were Frankenstein, and then she socked her. A couple of teachers jumped toward our table.

But Bunny started crying and put her arms around Mrs. Gangwhar's neck. I noticed the dark circles under Bunny's eyes. Why would Bunny have dark circles? I'd never known anyone my age to have them, and for as long as I knew her, she did. Every time I saw Bunny, which was in Sunday School or at Christian Science Camp in summer, her circles got darker and she kept getting bigger.

Luckily when she had that spell, Sunday School was almost over. Church ended upstairs and Mrs. Gangwhar walked Bunny like a giant puppet out of the room to take her to her parents. When I ran outside, my parents were talking with the Gillespis by their car. Bunny was inside it. The Gillespis looked like a dream — Gerri with her thick, red hair; pudgy Cy; all three of them smiling with dimples and healthy teeth. I had begun to study families. Smiles and gestures, I discovered, ran in families like freckles and hair color did. It's true, Cy *was* a good head shorter than Gerri, but such a prominent church member that no one seemed to find that strange.

"Well, Cy, it's a beautiful day for a drive," my mother said. I recognized it as an exit line. She crossed her arms and smiled sweetly. My father dug into the pocket of his white shirt for a Kent and slid one from its white flip top box. He took his Zippo from his trouser pocket. Its cap thonked open; the flint scraped against the strike wheel, the flame popped.

"Dad?" I said quickly.

He looked up and walked the flame over for me to blow it out. My father didn't know where to put Cy. His admiration was reserved for men of science, men who experimented with alloys and bonds, men who applied their expertise to the world's structural problems — fallen bridges, shattered pipe lines, mammoth, cracked containers. And so for a while he classified him as someone my mother had appointed for my continuing refinement.

My mother noticed I was just standing there, and that's when she said something about the new piano, and that's when Cy said, "Oh, gee," and poured his torso over his rigid knees and looked down at me and said, "And have we started lessons?"

I got a whiff of his hair cream, and my mother smiled and said, "No, we haven't yet, have we, Madelaine?" And then they got into their car with Bunny, as if everything were OK, just like it's supposed to be in Christian Science.

#

My grandmother bought me a piano. I should have seen it coming. I should have known from the way she'd begun to study me. "Why, Madelaine has piano hands," finding such pleasure in the observation that she repeated it for months in the same tone of startling discovery.

My hands were enormous. They dangled to my knees like an orangutan's. My palms faced backward. It seemed almost malicious that she would draw attention to them so. "Oh, Madelaine, don't be that way," she'd say when I pulled my hands back to sit on them. Her lips thinned with annoyance, but she persevered, and there it was one day, a Baldwin upright, sitting primly in our living room. My parents hoped that over time my playing would compliment the Persian throws and antique furniture with dilute Beethoven.

#

Cy's studio was in the corner of a tunnel one block deep, its length dotted with small shops. It ended in a T at the old Acme supermarket, and triangles of pale light fell on the damp cement from the stores. A venetian blind hung crookedly over the door's long window and a business card was tacked above the bell. It was a picture of a French poodle chewing on a quarter note.

The air was heavy in his studio and the walls were thick. There were no windows. I stared at the smudges on the yellow walls until they started throbbing. Cy walked toward us rubbing his hands around themselves as if he were putting on lotion. "So glad to see you Caroline, Maddie," he said, nodding at us in turn. His hands made a dry skin sound against each other.

My mother said, "OK, sweetie, I'll be back in forty-five minutes." I looked up at her pleadingly I guess, because she ran her finger down my arm and said, "Be good," and smiled at Cy and left me. The venetian blind jangled as the door closed, and Cy put his hands on my shoulders, his thumbs prodding me around the yellow screen that cut the room in half. The piano was yellow, too, a blond baby grand that rose up and floated in that yellow cubicle. The open top looked like a shark fin.

"Well, cupcake, let's make music," he said, and pulled the bench out. He sat beside me and the bench creaked. The temperature in the room shot up another ten degrees with the heat from his body. Every time he reached to turn a page, the bench creaked. His voice was thick and smooth. It lulled me, as the air of the room did, and suddenly I gasped.

"What's the matter?" he asked, jerking.

"I can't breathe," I said.

He got up and brought a miniature fan from behind the fin of the baby grand. It woke me up a little. He put his hands on my shoulders, his pudgy fingers worked them around and around. "Now, just relax," he said. "Here we concentrate on playing the piano. All we have to do first is work those fingers, and then we get to play all kinds of things."

He folded my hands in his and said, "Your hands are almost as big as mine," and his eyebrows made furry arches. "They are piano hands."

"Oh no they're not," I said, grabbing them back.

He looked as if I'd slapped him. "Everyone wants piano hands," he said.

"Not me," I said, nodding furiously and sliding them underneath me. I told him about my grandmother and ended up, "I didn't ask for a piano. If she would have asked me, I would have said the violin instead."

He made a face. He crushed his pudgy lips together, and crossed his eyes, and then looked down at me like that, and I couldn't help laughing. "Well, we'll find some way to make the piano almost as interesting as the violin," he said and leaned in closer. His breath was the same temperature as the room. It wasn't bitter like my father's breath from cigarettes, sour like my mother's from agitation. It was like a soft blanket, Cy's breath, like being indoors as the evening drains color from the sky before its icy, star-chipped blue.

#

The second year, Cy's studio, if possible, grew more airless. He changed his hair cream. It smelled stronger, and he changed his hair style, too, swooped it back from his low forehead in one serrated piece like rows in a newly plowed field. He'd gotten fatter. My musical tastes had not flourished under his tutelage. I was becoming downright schmaltzy. *Moon River* and *Volare* bracketed each day of my growing, the sentimental chord arrangements rising in my soul like sun-drenched hills.

I'd arrange myself tidily beside him as he wrote out the complicated chords onto creamy paper. His shoulder leaned against me while his right hand dribbled the chords across the page. I was too aware of Cy Gillespi's body. His soft lead pencil slid over the paper as he whispered, "Augmented. Diminished," pulling me down into a velvet eddy. I got all mixed up, confusing chord arrangements with algebraic formulas — G flat squared. I'd get all mixed up because twenty minutes into the lesson, it changed. Self-consciously, I'd be grinding out my lesson, my fingers leaving sweaty pads on the keys. He'd rise from the bench and go behind the fin of the piano. The lights would slowly dim. He'd reappear in back of me, rubbing his hands together. I'd continue pounding out *Moon River, Volare,* and then I'd feel his finger lightly on my neck. The back of it first, and then around the front, settling in the little dip underneath my

Adam's apple, and then inside my collar. I would feel his breath. He would have lowered his torso behind me. With his right arm, he'd reach in front, marking off the phrases. He would count softly in my ear, "And ah-1 and ah-2 and ah-3," like a purring metronome. I played on and on, my mistakes bold, my fingers dripping. I played. It would last forever. I'd come to my crashing conclusion, and then he'd sit down and play the whole piece from beginning to end flawlessly, and sometimes burst out singing. Then he'd take down a fresh four page folio of creamy paper and begin to scratch out new chords for next week's lesson. I couldn't make out the notes through all the blur. My heart was racing. My throat was dry. I came to associate learning with these dizzying sensations. And worse, the humming between my legs. It was like I was sitting on wires, and when Cy Gillespi got up to hit the switch, they crossed. By the time he draped himself over me, my wires had melted. When I walked out of his studio, the whole world looked electric.

#

From time to time, not frequently, my parents had to go away. The time I stayed with Bunny, it was some welding conference in Philadelphia. My mother said, "Sweetie, how would you like to stay the night with Bunny Gillespi?" and when I blinked and didn't say anything, she went on about how it would only be for the night, and then reminded me how much I liked Bunny and finally went on to tell me it was all settled anyhow. She'd talked to Gerri, and that was that. If you ask me, she could have cut it short by simply saying, "Dear, you're going to spend the night at Bunny's." As it was I was still swirling in the bogus world of choice, slowed only by the realization that there wasn't any.

She said also how this choice was very good, that Gerri herself had lived in Philadelphia for many years and she could tell me stories. I said I didn't think there would be time for that because of homework. Besides it was just for the night and if she needed to feel better about it, she could forget the Gillespis and let me stay at home by myself, thank you. I said I hated Cy Gillespi. She said that no, I didn't.

"How do you know?" I asked.

"Hate isn't nice," she answered.

#

I'd never been to their house. Bunny wasn't home from Swaine School yet, and Gerri showed me where to change out of my school dress into jeans. Then I asked Gerri could I help her. There were a few household chores I didn't feel stupid doing, like emptying dish washers and filling water glasses. She set down a pile of carrots and said, "Work on these." Her voice sounded far away. She sat down beside me and shredded my peeled carrots into a wooden bowl. Gerri's makeup was always perfect, unlike other Moms who by comparison appeared underdone or like they had to do it — a little powder on the nose to guard against shine, maybe some lipstick, the cheap kind, though, with dreadful names like peony or coral. Her lips were burgundy.

"I hope you like carrots, Maddie. There's not much in the house. I haven't had time to shop," she said.

"That's OK. Where's Bunny?" I asked.

"On her way home from school, with Cy. They should be home soon," she said. A weight fell across my heart when I thought of seeing him. Gerri drew her legs up underneath her. She had beautiful, long legs, probably from all those years in the theater. When she shifted position her stockings sighed. She hadn't taken off her suit jacket. It was cut to the waist, a white and blue checkered wool which she brightened with a wide red belt. I thought suddenly we might both be dreading Cy's return.

"Don't tell anyone," she whispered and nudged me with her elbow, "but I loathe cooking, in case you haven't guessed."

I hadn't, nor had I heard anyone say that word before, loathe — and she drew it out so it sounded British and funny. I giggled. "Loathe, simply loathe," she drew it out again.

"I loathe fish sticks," I said, laughing.

"And I simply loathe fruit cocktail with those little hard chunks of canned fruit."

"I loathe, simply loathe, the piano," I shrieked. "Oops, I didn't mean that," I said, looking down quickly at my pile of carrots.

Gerri touched me on the shoulders. "Relax," she said, "it's all right to loathe the piano. There aren't any rules here that say you have to like anything you don't. I loathe the piano, too. The only time I like the piano is when I put a record on, because then I can turn it off." And she hooted.

"Does Cy know?" I whispered.

She frowned. Her legs sighed again. She rose with the bowl of carrots. "Occasionally we discuss it," she said.

I wanted to get us back to giggling. I didn't know many married people and what went on between them, and if it looked as queer from the inside as it did from out here. I wanted to remind Gerri that she'd just said it was all right not to like what you do not like, but her silence was too heavy.

"Will Bunny be home soon?" I asked again.

"With Cy, any second."

I didn't know any other adults who tossed out first names that casually. If it had been my mother, she would have said, "She'll be arriving any minute with Mr. Gillespi," as if his first name were as private as his underpants. So when she said his name, it felt like I was pulled in much too close, and for all their queer formality, I started missing mom and dad.

"Why don't you put that stack of dishes out on the dining room table?" she asked, and then the front door opened. A look passed between us as voices from the outside tumbled in, roughing up what we'd established.

#

The kitchen door swung open, and Cy looked surprised. Something passed between the two adults — a squaring of the shoulders from him; her gaze, set into the middle distance. He wore the expression I'd seen after church when he stood among the old women sipping tea as if he were a little boy who should be outside playing with other little boys but for some reason had not learned how to. "Well, how-dee do," he said, walking to the sink rubbing his hands together. "How-dee do," he enunciated his pudgy lips at

Gerri, but it did not sound hearty. She leaned against the counter and looked at him, her head at an angle. "Well, gee," he said against her silence, and to me, "are you staying for dinner?"

"I'm sorry I forgot to tell you, Cy. The Stahls are away on business in Philadelphia. Maddie's going to spend the night with us." She stepped forward.

"Gee, honey, you know how I feel about surprises," he said, and scratched the back of his neck, squinting.

Gerri put a sauce pan on the burner and it began to smoke. "Oh," he cried.

"Relax," said Gerri, "it's just something I spilled on the unit here." Cy pushed his lips together and washed his hands again, this time for a long time, rolling them over and over.

"You could have cleaned it up," he said. I stared at his brown shoulders and then rolled against the door to go wait for Bunny in another room. Their voices sounded as if they were rehearsing for a play — stiff, sort of jerky, a lot of starts and then a bunch of words. I walked softly to the end of the living room away from the kitchen. There was a table full of family photographs. A studio portrait of Bunny — she is maybe three — shows her in a crisp pinafore, its straps perky and fresh as a butterfly's new wings. Ringlets descend from her glossy hair, parted in the middle. They frame her square little face. Her eyes slide away from the camera and on her lap is a very black kitten, propped, astonished, looking out into my eyes. Bunny looks in another direction. It is as if she is waiting to be told, "Pet the cat, darling," or "Loosen your grip. Kitty can't breathe." And there are the smudges, the dark circles under her eyes, even though the idea is proven by the picture of a happy little girl with her sweet little kitten. The circles don't belong there. They make that part of her a grown-up in some way, even though she's posed in ruffles, ankle socks, and Mary Janes.

I put the picture down. I didn't know I'd picked it up. I slid it around, trying to remember its angle against the other photographs.

#

It was a fuzzy, windowless dining room, and the carpet was yellow ochre, a color you'd choose if you had a lot of pets. I didn't see any, though. Bunny slurped a Coke. I was not hungry. When Bunny was not slurping, her face was in her plate, which was still empty. Cy said a stupid grace, "Our father, we thank thee for thy great bounty and our taking it together, um." We all stared at our plates and I wondered how we'd get through the dinner. Gerri tapped Bunny on the shoulder and she looked up. The circles under her eyes shone with a purple sheen. They were indentations, as if a pair of thumbs had been pressed hard into her sockets. When she smiled it was as if she'd done something bad — broken a dish and hidden the pieces.

"Sweetheart, what would you like?" Gerri asked her. Bunny made a face. She'd turned into a three-year-old, and I bit my lip thinking about getting through the whole evening with Bunny being three. And where would I sleep? I closed my eyes and saw Cy's chubby fingers. I knew his thumbs as well as I knew mine. Outside of his studio, in the world, even if the world was only the dining room of Cy and Gerri Gillespi, suddenly it felt all wrong.

Cy was waiting to be served. His lips were pursed so tightly, they made a yellow line. "Your daddy is in Philly at a conference. That's important stuff. What kind of a conference?" he asked.

"Welding," I said through a mouthful of French fries. They were mealy. I reached for my water glass but my hand shot past it and knocked it over.

"Never mind," said Gerri rising smoothly and reaching for my glass. "Sit still. I'll get you more water."

Cy helped himself to carrot salad with a sigh, and then speared three hamburger patties. "How are you coming with Mind over Matter?" he asked. I stared blankly.

"Mind over Matter," he repeated. "One of our basic Christian Science concepts. We've been over that, remember? Our minds can make us believe all sorts of things are happening that really aren't. We are continually engaged, whether in Sunday school or during our piano lessons, in discovering the truth. And learning to separate what really happened from what our minds make us think happened. You know how a sick mind can make a sick body." His muddy eyes softened even more.

"Isn't that so, lollipop?" he asked, patting the back of Bunny's head. She leaned away from him and scratched her shoulder. "I love teaching the piano particularly to my Christian Science pupils. We're on the same wave length. Students of the truth."

"Oh, yes," I said, my voice wavering. I wanted Gerri to burst through the swinging doors, a bucket of water held aloft in her strong arms to throw at Cy's talking.

"Students of the truth," he said coyly, as if at any moment he'd uncurl his fingers, and from the palm release licorice, Hershey kisses, nonpareils, thus signaling it was all a joke, a sweetness.

He smiled, grabbing his knife and fork and attacked a hamburger patty. He tore into it, his head sunken between his shoulders. Gerri returned with my glass of water, and the three of us stared at him in silence.

#

When Bunny asked to see my "jammies," I bristled. She'd bounced back from being the three-year-old of the dinner table, and now she wouldn't let me alone. I was trying to do my homework. Her room was pink, as screamingly pink as her father's studio was yellow. The curtains went from ceiling to floor like enormous gowns, their waists cinched in with fat, striped ribbons. They hung in front of a tiny, square window you had to stand on your toes to see out of.

"Oh, no, Dr. Denten's," she exclaimed.

"You got something better?" I asked, glaring.

She walked to her closet with enlarged dignity and pulled a night-gown off her hanger. "This," she said, holding it by the waist as if she was going to dance it around the bedroom. It was shiny, satiny, a light chocolate brown.

"You wear *that* to sleep in?" I asked. There was a big scoop where a neck would be and it had two cone-like shapes for breasts. I wondered if Bunny could fill them. It hadn't occurred to me to look out for Bunny's breasts. It hadn't occurred to me to do anything but dread the coming of my own. I spread my books on the floor. We were reading the diary of Samuel Pepys in English class.

"Have you begun yet?" she interrupted me, bouncing on the bed and holding the nightgown over her front. She smiled the dark-circled smile I'd noticed at dinner.

"Begun what?" I asked.

"Begun. You know. To develop," Bunny said.

There was a picture of Samuel Pepys at the front of the colonial America section and he looked like a reptile with a wig. I had peeked ahead in the section and everyone up to Emerson looked that way and I despaired, because I loved to read but the thought of reading men who looked like that totally depressed me. There was only one woman in that reader, and that was Emily Dickinson and she looked flat as a board and bloodless and then I knew what it was that Bunny was asking, it popped into my head with the image of Emily's flat chest and I said, "Oh, develop, like periods and stuff. Well, no. Have you?"

She smiled as if she had a whole box of chocolates hidden away somewhere and, turning away, slid on her nightgown. She was the only friend I knew who had a double bed.

"That night gown. Where did you get it?" I asked.

"Want to try it on?"

"No. I just wondered if it's your mom's," I said.

"Nope," she said. "My dad gave it to me."

"Your dad?" I asked. It seemed strange. My dad was still giving me things like microscopes and rocks, and that was fine with me. She got into her side of the bed and turned the light off.

"Hey, I wasn't ready," I said still down on the floor. There was a tiny silence in which the sudden darkness of the room spread out like a wave. I closed my reader and scraped my stuff together as best I could.

"Have you ever done it?" Bunny asked.

"Done what?" I asked, feeling my way up into bed. "You know, 'it.' Done 'it' with anyone?"

I began to get the willies. I turned down the covers on my side and thought I felt the temperature on hers go up. "Of course not," I answered.

"But I bet you wanted to," she taunted.

I felt something knock against my arm. I jerked. Bunny laughed sharply. "What are you doing?" I asked.

"It's just my hair brush," she said softly.

"You bring your brush to bed?"

"It's just my brush," she repeated. "Do you want to hold it?"

"Why would I want to hold your brush?" I asked. "I brought my own."

"But this one's special. If you do what I say, I'll let you hold it, too."

"What's the big deal about a hair brush?"

"It goes inside me," she said.

I didn't have an answer for that. I was thinking suddenly of Coca Cola. I was thinking of all the times I drank it on my Grandmother's back yard stoop, sitting there on hot summer days after huge Sunday dinners. I was thinking of all the Coca Colas drunk at Mr. Crawford's riding farm, after a couple of hours in the ring and then cooling the horses down and putting them back in their stalls, and then running into the tiny, square tack room for our ice cold Cokes. The machine was red and round shouldered and the bottles would thonk their way down after the machine ate your dime. Yes. I wanted a Coca Cola. "Is it too late for a Coke?" I asked.

I felt the brush on my arm again, this time stroking. I jerked away. "There's school tomorrow," I said, "let's just go to sleep."

She slid closer. "A brush can be a lot of fun," she said. I couldn't imagine. I couldn't picture much of anything at thirteen. I was scared. It was dark. She started moaning.

"Bunny, what is it?" I said, thinking she might be having one of her spells.

"The hair brush. Try it," she said breathlessly.

Then it was in my hand. I held it underneath the covers. Her hand encircled mine and drew it to her side. Her night gown was up around her hips. The skin was warm and silky, dry and hot. Her legs slid open and it was like a furnace there. She moaned again. "Put it there, put it there," she said. I didn't have to do a thing. She did it. She put my hand and the brush on her belly and brushed downward. Her stomach was soft and warm. I started giggling.

"You can't brush peoples' stomachs, Bunny," I said. She lowered it on her. I thought I felt a few stiff hairs and with that, grabbed my hand back and pretended to be a board. She fumbled for the brush and resumed moaning.

"It goes inside me. Want to see?" she said.

"No," I answered quickly. "You go ahead." I felt sick. It was dark. I was hot. I'd begun to sweat right through my Dr. Denten's. I turned away from her. There was a rhythm she was making, a swaying that I couldn't picture. I hung my arm out over the side of the bed. She moaned for a while. I couldn't imagine the hair brush inside her. How would it go? Wouldn't the bristles hurt? How could they possibly go up her? What would the pleasure be of an old, bristly brush up inside your privates?

#

"Well, dear, how was your overnight with Bunny?" my mother asked.

"Fine, Mom," I said. My stomach clenched, and I stopped chewing. It was dinner time. My father was in his feeding mode, his head six inches from his plate. She was trying to train him to slow down and enjoy dinner as the time for family sharing. She had to remind him with broad cues, like setting down her knife and fork and pushing her chair back from the table and asking slowly, "Well, Charles, how was your day at Lehigh?" But they must have had a good time in Philadelphia, because she was letting him have his head with the mashed potatoes. "Gerri fixed hamburgers, Mom, and French fries."

"You must say, 'Mrs. Gillespi.' It isn't right for you to call a grown-up by her first name. Did you finish your homework?"

"Most of it, Mom. I didn't get to the math. Nobody at Bunny's knew algebra."

The talk shifted from that to school, and what my algebra teacher had to say about my incomplete assignment, and how my father would help me after dinner, wouldn't he, dear? and we slipped away from the Gillespis, my mother content with the details allowed her. After my night at the Gillespi's, I felt dirty and confused. I wanted nothing to do with Bunny. I told Mom we'd had an argument, and that I didn't like her anymore. I told her she shoplifted and chewed gum in public. I told her she had a secret stash of super hero comics. Meanwhile, I began to read every Harold Robbins novel I could get my hands on. My grades fell, which was disastrous, because they were never high. And then one day I said to my mother, "I'm not going to take piano lessons anymore. I'm not going back to Cy Gillespis." But my mother insisted. Practicing became a battleground. She thought adolescence had officially begun and resigned herself to battle.

Cy regressed me from bebop and pop tunes to simplified versions of the classics, hoping, I guess, to instill a basic rhythm to my shaky grasp of music. He said he'd never seen anyone so totally lacking in rhythm. I couldn't get the hang of any other timing than 4-4. It scrambled my brain and when the left hand had to pound out a different timing from the right, it was worse than trying to sit on a horse with a wobbly canter. No, I had no rhythm. I'd stiffened up inside.

Our lessons developed. He'd conclude them with the Christian Science weekly lesson, and we'd read the selections from his Bible and Science and Health. He'd refer to this as "our little talk with God and Mary Baker Eddy." The solid aphorisms — "Overcome evil with good," and "Mind over matter," — reverberated in the cauldron of my psyche. As we read out loud together, Cy would reach for my big hand. He'd cover it with his fat one and guide it rhythmically over his trousered thigh.

#

One night after my mother said, "Good night," and after prayers, I climbed down the rose trellis outside my bedroom window and walked with thrilling alertness across the silent town. I paused before the archway of the Acme Arcade. Its funnel of damp air made me shiver. A car turned over the top of the hill onto Main Street, and I slipped inside the darkness before the head lights could frame me. I walked through the vaulted, brick tunnel and out into the parking lot, and found a small mound of broken bricks and chipped mortar. I picked up a brick. I was breathing as if finally I'd discovered rhythm. It was a starry night; a tipped moon made a tear in the indigo, and a cat flew from one side of the lot to the other. I caught my breath. My wool scarf itched me underneath my chin.

I walked back inside the tunnel. When I reached his studio, I lit a match. The flame flickered on the poodle and the quarter note. I centered myself in front of the door and backed up the five steps to the opposite wall. I threw the match down and let my eyes adjust to the blackness. I thought of Cy Gillespi's hands, and raised the brick. I thought of his furry breath and his milk-chocolate eyes that translated his adult heat into such confusing kindness, and I thought of the complicated notes scratched across the creamy pages, and of his yellow walls and blond piano, and I thought of his body, square and round at the same time, and I thought of Bunny. I was afraid that just by breathing the air in Cy Gillespi's studio I'd get dark circles, too. I was as certain of this as I was of other things, like knowing I'd never stop biting my nails, especially the skin around them, even though my grandmother assured me this would cause cancer. I would simply die if I had one more lesson. First I'd get fat, and under my eyes would be the dark circles. They would come gradually at first and then darken to a Concord grape purple and start to shine, the skin around my eyes textured differently from my nose and cheeks. Then I, too, would be made a Gillespi. He would have staked his claim so gradually that my parents would not have noticed and this was because Cy Gillespi had transferred his awful weight onto me, onto the two of us, now. I imagined him entering Bunny's bedroom when she was asleep, at least when he thought she was. She would not open her eyes. Into her room I saw him coming, a little light spilling under the curtains where the bottoms didn't quite touch the floor, and he would stand, rubbing his hands ever so softly. Then he would lower himself over his thick middle and spill himself onto the bed on top of the covers. He would lie on her like an extra blanket and smooth both sides as far as his arms could reach and he would call this, "tucking in." She might wake up, if she had been asleep, and say, "Daddy, I can't breathe. Get off me," and he wouldn't or would. I could never know, as I couldn't know any of this, either. I just knew I couldn't go back. Every time I thought of him, I stopped breathing.

I raised the brick. The crashing glass pulled me back into the real life of the night, and my heart jumped, catapulting me from the tunnel out to the parking lot. I ran through the maze of sleeping alleys.

#

I flew invincible, my high tops fleet, the air fresh and bathed and piney. Leaves on the asphalt from a recent rain were a brilliant mosaic, and I had enough mind to set my feet firmly, it was that slick. My body felt long and clean and I could have run for hours. I decided once and for all to scrap the piano and take up sports, and maybe ask my parents for a horse again and get a Saturday job mucking stalls at Crawford's to help pay for it. I was rehearsing the request in my mind as I climbed back up the trellis to my room, and it only struck me odd in retrospect that all the lights were burning.

"Young lady, I think you better tell us where you were."

They were sitting on the edge of my bed. She looked spent. He looked weary. He didn't have his glasses on, and so he also looked undressed. The back of his head was disheveled. "Where in the name of God have you been?" Upset didn't become him. It made his body awkward and his Adam's apple bob. His upset didn't sound convincing. It sounded like he'd picked up the language from old movies but had neither the skill nor the heart for intonation. A slide whistle, nevertheless, plunged from my heart to my crotch and back up again. My sweater smelled like the wind.

"Uh oh," I said.

"What in the world…?" my father gasped. He was beside himself. I don't think it was with worry so much as with chagrin. His muscles and joints weren't programmed for surprises. He didn't know where to put this piece of my behavior, in spite of our sharing many television hours in which we'd root for Robin Hood and Zorro, who had both definitely loomed in my mind that night.

"I broke the window on Cy Gillespi's door," I faltered.

My mother had a grid of worry on her face. She let my father rant and sat on the bed with her hands folded and her lips puffy. She could have been nodding internally to his points, or she could have been steeping in an upset all her own, because suddenly she cut him off and said, "I am certainly not going to tell Grammy about this. It would break her heart. It would just break her heart to pieces."

But I told them. I sort of yanked it out.

My mother received the information as if she were cement and my words sprays of gravel thrown against her. She sat rigidly, hands clasped. I dropped my words into the well of their silence and soon almost stopped believing that the terrible lessons and the hair brush night had happened, and wondered if they weren't the manifest flaw in my Christian Science. After all, Christian Science said that our bodies were *thought,* and good and evil played through them, and wouldn't the reverse be true, that if our bodies were evil, then our minds would ooze all sorts of evil thoughts? Maybe my evil mind had made the whole thing up. Maybe I'd made up even Cy Gillespi's furry, suffocating charm. The whole thing made me want to hold my breath until I reached the safer shore of twenty-one, when I'd have built an arsenal of answers.

My father leaned exhausted in the doorway. His lips were slack, the corners down like a fish. "Poppycock!" suddenly he thundered. "Where did you get such ideas?" He had interrupted me as I was choking out the part about Cy's fingers in my blouse. I gulped.

"What?" I said. "What?"

"How do you come up with such nonsense?" he said, his body tall and rigid. I thought he was going to jerk across the bed and hit me. I was in front of the window still.

"Close the window, hon," my mother said. I turned and closed the window.

"Pull down the shade," she said.

My father's voice cut in. "I have never heard anything so…." But I didn't hear my father's word that was about to describe the contents of my confession. A hundred pounds of sleep had fallen on my shoulders. I fished behind my eyes for the sensation of tears, but there weren't any. I wasn't going to continue to press my version. I knew that much. My experience had dwindled into a version of the truth.

"Madelaine, this is very serious, and I want you to know how serious this is. There will be no horse back riding lessons at Crawford's until, until…"

My mouth fell open. "That's not fair!" But my wail flew across to a door frame empty of my father. He'd made his judgment. He left the messy scene for bed.

My mother was clicking the shapely tips of her thumb nails and looking down. She lifted her face. Her eyes closed momentarily, and then she opened them, deeply saddened, and said, "Honey, why didn't you tell me sooner?"

Everyone Is...

Beth Bailey

"Everyone is born naked and after that,
everything is drag."—*RuPaul*

I was young.
The way my heart didn't quicken
should have been the tip off.
How I was about to embark
didn't occur to me.

All I said was,
"If you were going to kiss someone,
who would it be?"
And I was picturing
Katherine Hepburn or Nancy Drew.
Or maybe, my eighth grade Spanish teacher.

My friend was looking at me, saying,
drumroll please
"I'd like to kiss
social conventions please
well, I guess that guy, Brad, on the soccer team.
heterosexuality please
The blond one with a scar on his arm"

And, suddenly, the universe wasn't big enough
to hold me anymore.
I tried again,
"Yes. But, I was talking about a *girl*.
What girl would you like to kiss?"
Now, my nakedness was complete.

Oh, Mother, highlighting sections of the Bible
and brandishing them like hot irons;
don't take my name in vain,
don't take my history away
don't tell me what I already know, but can't believe.

Oh, my peers; don't refuse to admit me.
I'm already there.
I have thought about my place in life
more than you would ever dare.

Oh, Principal, don't make me a laboratory rat
for the school psychologist.
An inkblot's just an inkblot.
A kiss is just a kiss.

I do remember this,
lying down in my buzzing garden;
watching the sides of strawberries
changing from green hardness to summer red
dangling between sky and earth,
just like I did.

A Question of Class

Dorothy Allison

The first time I heard, "They're different than us, don't value human life the way we do," I was in high school in Central Florida. The man speaking was an army recruiter talking to a bunch of boys, telling them what the army was really like, what they could expect overseas. A cold angry feeling swept over me. I had heard the word *they* pronounced in that same callous tone before. *They*, those people over there, those people who are not us, they die so easily, kill each other so casually. They are different. *We*, I thought. *Me*.

When I was six or eight back in Greenville, South Carolina, I had heard that same matter-of-fact tone of dismissal applied to me. "Don't you play with her. I don't want you talking to them." Me and my family, we had always been *they*. Who am I? I wondered, listening to that recruiter. Who are my people? We die so easily, disappear so completely — we/they, the poor and the queer. I pressed my bony white trash fists to my stubborn lesbian mouth. The rage was a good feeling, stronger and purer than the shame that followed it, the fear and the sudden urge to run and hide, to deny, to pretend I did not know who I was and what the world would do to me.

My people were not remarkable. We were ordinary, but even so we were mythical. We were the *they* everyone talks about — the ungrateful poor. I grew up trying to run away from the fate that destroyed so many of the people I loved, and having learned the habit of hiding, I found I had also learned to hide from myself. I did not know who I was, only that I did not want to be *they*, the ones who are destroyed or dismissed to make the "real" people, the important people, feel safer. By the time I understood that I was queer, that habit of hiding was deeply set in me, so deeply that it was not a choice, but an instinct. Hide, hide to survive, I thought, knowing that if I told the truth about my life, my family, my sexual desire, my history, I would move over into that unknown territory, the land of they, would never have the chance to name my own life, to understand it or claim it.

Why are you so afraid? my lovers and friends have asked me the many times I have suddenly seemed a stranger, someone who would not speak to them, would not do the things they believed I should do, simple things like applying for a job, or a grant, or some award they were sure I could acquire easily. Entitlement, I have told them, is a matter of feeling like we rather than they. You think you have a right to things, a place in the world, and it is so intrinsically a part of you that you cannot imagine people like me, people who seem to live in your world, who don't have it. I have explained what I know over and over, in every way I can, but I have never been able to make clear the degree of my fear, the extent to which I feel myself denied: not only that I am queer in a world that hates queers, but that I was born poor into a world that despises the poor. The need to make my world believable to people who have never experienced it is a part of why I write fiction. I know that some things must be felt to be understood, that despair, for example, can never be adequately analyzed; it must be lived. But if I can write a story that so draws the reader in that she imagines herself like my character, feels their sense of fear and uncertainty, their hopes and terrors, then I have come closer to knowing myself as real, important as the very people I have always watched with awe.

#

I have known I was a lesbian since I was a teenager, and I have spent a good twenty years making peace with the effects of incest and physical abuse. But what may be the central fact of my life is that I was born in 1949 in Greenville, South Carolina, the bastard daughter of a white woman from a desperately poor family, a girl who had left the seventh grade the year before, worked as a waitress, and was just a month past fifteen when she had me. That fact, the inescapable impact of being born in a condition of poverty that this society finds shameful, contemptible, and somehow deserved, has had dominion over me to such an extent that I have spent my life trying to overcome or deny it. I have learned with great difficulty that the vast majority of people believe that poverty is a voluntary condition.

I have loved my family so stubbornly that every impulse to hold them in contempt has sparked in me a countersurge of pride — complicated and undercut by an urge to fit us into the acceptable myths and theories of both mainstream society and a lesbian-feminist reinterpretation. The choice becomes Steven Spielberg movies or Erskine Caldwell novels, the one valorizing and the other caricaturing, or the patriarchy as villain, trivializing the choices the men and women of my family have made. I have had to fight broad generalizations from every theoretical viewpoint.

Traditional feminist theory has had a limited understanding of class differences and of how sexuality and self are shaped by both desire and denial. The ideology implies we are all sisters who should only turn our anger and suspicion on the world outside the lesbian community. It is easy to say that the patriarchy did it, that poverty and social contempt are products of the world of the fathers, and often I felt a need to collapse my sexual history into what I was willing to share of my class background, to pretend that my life both as a lesbian and as a working-class escapee was constructed by the patriarchy. Or conversely, to ignore how much my life was shaped by growing up poor and talk only about what incest did to my identity as a woman and as a lesbian. The difficulty is that I can't attribute everything that has been problematic about my life simply and easily to the patriarchy, or to incest, or even to the invisible and much denied class structure of our society.

In my lesbian-feminist collective we had long conversations about the mind/body split, the way we compartmentalize our lives to survive. For years I thought that that concept referred to the way I had separated my activist life from the passionate secret life in which I acted on my sexual desires. I was convinced that the fracture was fairly simple, that it would be healed when there was time and clarity to do so — at about the same point when I might begin to understand sex. I never imagined that it was not a split but a splintering, and I passed whole portions of my life — days, months, years — in pure directed progress, getting up every morning and setting to work, working so hard and so continually that I avoided examining in any way what I knew about my life. Busywork became a trance state. I ignored who I really was and how I became that person, continued in that daily progress, became an automaton who was what she did.

I tried to become one with the lesbian-feminist community so as to feel real and valuable. I did not know that I was hiding, blending in for safety just as I had done in high school, in college. I did not recognize the impulse to forget. I believed that all those things I did not talk about, or even let myself think too much about, were not important, that none of them defined me. I had constructed a life, an identity in which I took pride, an alternative lesbian family in which I felt safe, and I did not realize that the fundamental me had almost disappeared.

It is surprising how easy it was to live that life. Everyone and everything cooperated with the process. Everything in our culture — books, television, movies, school, fashion — is presented as if it is being seen by one pair of eyes, shaped by one set of hands, heard by one pair of ears. Even if you know you are not part of that imaginary creature — if you like country music not symphony, read books cynically, listen to the news unbelievingly, are lesbian not heterosexual, and surround yourself with your own small deviant community — you are still shaped by that hegemony, or your resistance to it. The only way I found to resist that homogenized view of the world was to make myself part of something larger than myself. As a feminist and a radical lesbian organizer, and later as a sex radical (which eventually became the term, along with pro-sex feminist, for those who were not anti-pornography but anti-censorship, those of us arguing for sexual diversity), the need to belong, to feel safe, was just as important for me as for any heterosexual, nonpolitical citizen, and sometimes even more important because the rest of my life was so embattled.

The first time I read the Jewish lesbian Irena Klepfisz's poems,[†] I experienced a frisson of recognition. It was not that my people had been "burned off the map" or murdered as hers had. No, we had been encouraged to destroy ourselves, made invisible because we did not fit the myths of the noble poor generated by the middle class. Even now, past forty and stubbornly proud of my family, I feel the draw of that mythology, that romanticized, edited version of the poor. I find myself looking back and wondering what was real, what was true. Within my family, so much was lied about, joked about, denied, or told with deliberate indirection, an undercurrent of humiliation or a brief pursed grimace that belied everything that had been said. What was real? The poverty depicted in books and movies was romantic, a backdrop for the story of how it was escaped.

The poverty portrayed by left-wing intellectuals was just as romantic, a platform for assailing the upper and middle classes, and from their perspective, the working-class hero was invariably male, righteously indignant, and inhumanly noble. The reality of self-hatred and violence was either absent or caricatured. The poverty I knew was dreary, deadening, shameful, the women powerful in ways not generally seen as heroic by the world outside the family.

My family's lives were not on television, not in books, not even comic books. There was a myth of the poor in this country, but it did not include us, no matter how hard I tried to squeeze us in. There was an idea of good poor — hard-working, ragged but clean, and intrinsically honorable. I understood that we were the bad poor: men who drank and couldn't keep a job; women, invariably pregnant before marriage, who quickly became worn, fat, and old from working too many hours and bearing too many children; and children with runny noses, watery eyes, and the wrong attitudes. My cousins quit school, stole cars, used drugs, and took dead-end jobs pumping gas or waiting tables. We were not noble, not grateful, not even hopeful. We knew ourselves despised. My family was ashamed of being poor, of feeling hopeless. What was there to work for, to save money for, to fight for or struggle against? We had generations before us to teach us that nothing ever changed, and that those who did try to escape failed.

My mama had eleven brothers and sisters, of whom I can name only six. No one is left alive to tell me the names of the others. It was my grandmother who told me about my real daddy, a shiftless pretty man who was supposed to have married, had six children, and sold cut-rate life insurance to poor Black people. My mama married when I was a year old, but her husband died just after my little sister was born a year later.

When I was five, Mama married the man she lived with until she died. Within the first year of their marriage Mama miscarried, and while we waited out in the hospital parking lot, my stepfather molested me for the first time, something he continued to do until I was past thirteen. When I was eight or so, Mama took us away to a motel after my stepfather beat me so badly it caused a family scandal, but we returned after two weeks. Mama told me that she really had no choice: she could not support us alone. When I was eleven I told one of my cousins that my stepfather was molesting me. Mama packed up my sisters and me and took us away for a few days, but again, my stepfather swore he would stop, and again we went back after a few weeks. I stopped talking for a while, and I have only vague memories of the next two years.

My stepfather worked as a route salesman, my mama as a waitress, laundry worker, cook, or fruit packer. I could never understand, since they both worked so hard and such long hours, how we never had enough money, but it was also true of my mama's brothers and sisters who worked hard in the mills or the furnace industry. In fact, my parents did better than anyone else in the family. But eventually my stepfather was fired and we hit bottom — nightmarish months of marshals at the door, repossessed furniture, and rubber checks. My parents worked out a scheme so that it appeared my stepfather had abandoned us, but instead he went down to Florida, got a new job, and rented us a house. He returned with a U-Haul trailer in the dead of night, packed us up, and moved us south.

The night we left South Carolina for Florida, my mama leaned over the back seat of her old Pontiac and promised us girls, "It'll be better there." I don't know if we believed her, but I remember crossing Georgia in the early morning, watching the red clay hills and swaying gray blankets of moss recede through the back window. I kept looking at the trailer behind us, ridiculously small to contain everything we owned. Mama had packed nothing that wasn't fully paid off, which meant she had only two things of worth: her washing and sewing machines, both of them tied securely to the trailer walls. Throughout the trip I fantasized an accident that would burst that trailer, scattering old clothes and cracked dishes on the tarmac.

I was only thirteen. I wanted us to start over completely, to begin again as new people with nothing of the past left over. I wanted to run away from who we had been seen to be, who we had been. That desire is one I have seen in other members of my family. It is the first thing I think of when trouble comes — the geographic solution. Change your name, leave town, disappear, make yourself over. What hides behind that impulse is the conviction that the life you have lived, the person you are, is valueless, better off abandoned, that running away is easier than trying to change things, that change itself is not possible. Sometimes I think it is this conviction — more seductive than alcohol or violence, more subtle than sexual hatred or gender injustice — that has dominated my life and made real change so painful and difficult.

Moving to Central Florida did not fix our lives. It did not stop my stepfather's violence, heal my shame, or make my mother happy. Once there, our lives became controlled by my mother's illness and medical bills. She had a hysterectomy when I was about eight and endured a series of hospitalizations for ulcers and a chronic back problem. Through most of my adolescence she superstitiously refused to allow anyone to mention the word *cancer*. When she was not sick, Mama and my stepfather went on working, struggling to pay off what seemed an insurmountable load of debts.

By the time I was fourteen, my sisters and I had found ways to discourage most of our stepfather's sexual advances. We were not close, but we united against him. Our efforts were helped along when he was referred to a psychotherapist after he lost his temper at work, and was prescribed drugs that made him sullen but less violent. We were growing up quickly, my sisters moving toward dropping out of school while I got good grades and took every scholarship exam I could find. I was the first person in my family to graduate from high school, and the fact that I went on to college was nothing short of astonishing.

We all imagine our lives are normal, and I did not know my life was not everyone's. It was in Central Florida that I began to realize just how different we were. The people we met there had not been shaped by the rigid class structure that dominated the South Carolina Piedmont. The first time I looked around my junior high classroom and realized I did not know who those people were — not only as individuals but as categories, who their people were and how they saw themselves — I also realized that they did not know me. In Greenville, everyone knew my family, knew we were trash, and that meant we were supposed to be poor, supposed to have grim low-paid jobs, have babies in our teens, and never finish school. But Central Florida in the 1960s was full of runaways and immigrants, and our mostly white working-class suburban school sorted us out not by income and family background but by intelligence and aptitude tests. Suddenly I was boosted into the college-bound track, and while there was plenty of contempt for my inept social skills, pitiful wardrobe, and slow drawling accent, there was also something I had never experienced before: a protective anonymity, and a kind of grudging respect and curiosity about who I might become. Because they did not see poverty and hopelessness as a foregone conclusion for my life, I could begin to imagine other futures for myself.

In that new country, we were unknown. The myth of the poor settled over us and glamorized us. I saw it in the eyes of my teachers, the Lion's Club representative who paid for my new glasses, and the lady from the Junior League who told me about the scholarship

I had won. Better, far better, to be one of the mythical poor than to be part of the they I had known before. I also experienced a new level of fear, a fear of losing what had never before been imaginable. Don't let me lose this chance, I prayed, and lived in terror that I might suddenly be seen again as what I knew myself to be.

#

As an adolescent I thought that my family's escape from South Carolina played like a bad movie. We fled the way runaway serfs might have done, with the sheriff who would have arrested my stepfather the imagined border guard. I am certain that if we had remained in South Carolina, I would have been trapped by my family's heritage of poverty, jail, and illegitimate children — that even being smart, stubborn, and a lesbian would have made no difference.

My grandmother died when I was twenty, and after Mama went home for the funeral, I had a series of dreams in which we still lived up in Greenville just down the road from where Granny died. In the dreams I had two children and only one eye, lived in a trailer, and worked at the textile mill. Most of my time was taken up with deciding when I would finally kill my children and myself. The dreams were so vivid, I became convinced they were about the life I was meant to have had, and I began to work even harder to put as much distance as I could between my family and me. I copied the dress, mannerisms, attitudes, and ambitions of the girls I met in college, changing or hiding my own tastes, interest, and desires. I kept my lesbianism a secret, forming a relationship with an effeminate male friend that served to shelter and disguise us both. I explained to friends that I went home so rarely because my stepfather and I fought too much for me to be comfortable in his house. But that was only part of the reason I avoided home, the easiest reason. The truth was that I feared the person I might become in my mama's house, the woman of my dreams — hateful, violent, and hopeless.

It is hard to explain how deliberately and thoroughly I ran away from my own life. I did not forget where I came from, but I gritted my teeth and hid it. When I could not get enough scholarship money to pay for graduate school, I spent a year of rage working as a salad girl, substitute teacher, and maid. I finally managed to find a job by agreeing to take any city assignment where the Social Security Administration needed a clerk. Once I had a job and my own place far away from anyone in my family, I became sexually and politically active, joining the Women's Center support staff and falling in love with a series of middle-class women who thought my accent and stories thoroughly charming. The stories I told about my family, about South Carolina, about being poor itself, were all lies, carefully edited to seem droll or funny. I knew damn well that no one would want to hear the truth about poverty, the hopelessness and fear, the feeling that nothing I did would ever make any difference and the raging resentment that burned beneath my jokes. Even when my lovers and I formed an alternative lesbian family, sharing what we could of our resources, I kept the truth about my background and who I knew myself to be a carefully obscured mystery. I worked as hard as I could to make myself a new person, an emotionally healthy radical lesbian activist, and I believed completely that by remaking myself I was helping to remake the world.

#

For a decade, I did not go home for more than a few days at a time. When in the 1980s I ran into the concept of feminist sexuality, I genuinely did not know what it meant. Though I was, and am, a feminist, and committed to claiming the right to act on my sexual desires without tailoring my lust to a sex-fearing society, demands that I explain or justify my sexual fantasies have left me at a loss. How does anyone explain sexual need?

The Sex Wars are over, I've been told, and it always makes me want to ask who won. But my sense of humor may be a little obscure to women who have never felt threatened by the way most lesbians use and mean the words *pervert* and *queer*. I use the word queer to mean more than lesbian. Since I first used it in 1980 I have always meant it to imply that I am not only a lesbian but a transgressive lesbian — femme, masochistic, as sexually aggressive as the women I seek out, and as pornographic in my imagination and sexual activities as the heterosexual hegemony has ever believed.

My aunt Dot used to joke, "There are two or three things I know for sure, but never the same things and I'm never as sure as I'd like." What I know for sure is that class, gender, sexual preference, and prejudice — racial, ethnic, and religious — form an intricate lattice that restricts and shapes our lives, and that resistance to hatred is not a simple act. Claiming your identity in the caldron of hatred and resistance to hatred is infinitely complicated, and worse, almost unexplainable.

I know that I have been hated as a lesbian both by "society" and by the intimate world of my extended family, but I have also been hated or held in contempt (which is in some ways more debilitating and slippery than hatred) by lesbians for behavior and sexual practices shaped in large part by class. My sexual identity is intimately constructed by my class and regional background, and much of the hatred directed at my sexual preference is class hatred — however much people, feminists in particular, like to pretend this is not a factor. The kind of woman I am attracted to is invariably the kind of woman who embarrasses respectably middle-class, politically aware lesbian feminists. My sexual ideal is butch, exhibitionistic, physically aggressive, smarter than she wants you to know, and proud of being called a pervert. Most often she is working class, with an aura of danger and an ironic sense of humor. There is a lot of contemporary lip service paid to sexual tolerance, but the fact that my sexuality is constructed within, and by, a butch/femme and leather fetishism is widely viewed with distaste or outright hatred.

For most of my life I have been presumed to be misguided, damaged by incest and childhood physical abuse, or deliberately indulging in hateful and retrograde sexual practices out of a selfish concentration on my own sexual satisfaction. I have been expected to abandon my desires, to become the normalized woman who flirts with fetishization, who plays with gender roles and treats the historical categories of deviant desire with humor or gentle contempt but never takes any of it so seriously as to claim a sexual identity based on these categories. It was hard enough for me to shake off demands when they were made by straight society. It was appalling when I found the same demands made by other lesbians.

One of the strengths I derive from my class background is that I am accustomed to contempt. I know that I have no chance of becoming what my detractors expect of me, and I believe that even the attempt to please them will only further engage their contempt, and my own self-contempt as well. Nonetheless, the relationship between the life I have lived and the way that life is seen by strangers has constantly invited a kind of self-mythologizing fantasy. It has always been tempting for me to play off of the stereotypes and misconceptions of mainstream culture, rather than describe a difficult and sometimes painful reality.

#

I am trying to understand how we internalize the myths of our society even as we resist them. I have felt a powerful temptation to write about my family as a kind of morality tale, with us as the heroes and middle and upper classes the villains. It would be within the romantic myth, for example, to pretend that we were the kind of noble Southern whites portrayed in the movies, mill workers for generations until driven out by alcoholism and a family propensity for rebellion and union talk. But that would be a lie. The truth is that no one in my family ever joined a union.

Taken to its limits, the myth of the poor would make my family over into union organizers or people broken by the failure of the unions. As far as my family was concerned, union organizers, like preachers, were of a different class, suspect and hated however much they might be admired for what they were supposed to be trying to achieve. Nominally Southern Baptist, no one in my family actually paid much attention to preachers, and only little children went to Sunday school. Serious belief in anything — any political ideology, any religious system, or any theory of life's meaning and purpose — was seen as unrealistic. It was an attitude that bothered me a lot when I started reading the socially conscious novels I found in the paperback racks when I was eleven or so. I particularly loved Sinclair Lewis's novels and wanted to imagine my own family as part of the working man's struggle.

"We were not joiners," my aunt Dot told me with a grin when I asked her about the union. My cousin Butch laughed at that, told me the union charged dues, and said, "Hell, we can't even be persuaded to toss money in the collection plate. An't gonna give it to no union man." It shamed me that the only thing my family wholeheartedly believed in was luck and the waywardness of fate. They held the dogged conviction that the admirable and wise thing to do was keep a sense of humor, never whine or cower, and trust that luck might someday turn as good as it had been bad — and with just as much reason. Becoming a political activist with an almost religious fervor was the thing I did that most outraged my family and the Southern working-class community they were part of.

Similarly, it was not my sexuality, my lesbianism, that my family saw as most rebellious; for most of my life, no one but my mama took my sexual preference very seriously. It was the way I thought about work, ambition, and self-respect. They were waitresses, laundry workers, counter girls. I was the one who went to work as a maid, something I never told any of them. They would have been angry if they had known. Work was just work for them, necessary. You did what you had to do to survive. They did not so much believe in taking pride in doing your job as in stubbornly enduring hard work and hard times. At the same time, they held that there were some forms of work, including maid's work, that were only for Black people, not white, and while I did not share that belief, I knew how intrinsic it was to the way my family saw the world. Sometimes I felt as if I straddled cultures and belonged on neither side. I would grind my teeth at what I knew was my family's unquestioning racism while continuing to respect their pragmatic endurance. But more and more as I grew older, what I felt was a deep estrangement from their view of the world, and gradually a sense of shame that would have been completely incomprehensible to them.

"Long as there's lunch counters, you can always find work," I was told by my mother and my aunts. Then they'd add, "I can get me a little extra with a smile." It was obvious there was supposed to be nothing shameful about it, that needy smile across a lunch counter, that rueful grin when you didn't have rent, or the half-provocative, half-pleading way my mama could cajole the man at the store to give her a little credit. But I hated it, hated the need for it and the shame that would follow every time I did it myself. It was begging, as far as I was concerned, a quasi-prostitution that I despised even while I continued to rely on it. After all, I needed the money.

"Just use that smile," my girl cousins used to joke, and I hated what I knew they meant. After college, when I began to support myself and study feminist theory, I became more contemptuous rather than more understanding of the women in my family. I told myself that prostitution is a skilled profession and my cousins were never more than amateurs. There was a certain truth in this, though like all cruel judgments rendered from the outside, it ignored the conditions that made it true. The women in my family, my mother included, had sugar daddies, not johns, men who slipped them money because they needed it so badly. From their point of view they were nice to those men because the men were nice to them, and it was never so direct or crass an arrangement that they would set a price on their favors. Nor would they have described what they did as prostitution. Nothing made them angrier than the suggestion that the men who helped them out did it just for their favors. They worked for a living, they swore, but this was different.

I always wondered if my mother hated her sugar daddy or if not him then her need for what he offered her, but it did not seem to me in memory that she had. He was an old man, half-crippled, hesitant and needy, and he treated my mama with enormous consideration and, yes, respect. The relationship between them was painful, and since she and my stepfather could not earn enough to support the family, Mama could not refuse her sugar daddy's money. At the same time the man made no assumptions about that money buying any-thing Mama was not already offering. The truth was, I think, that she genuinely liked him, and only partly because he treated her so well.

Even now, I am not sure whether there was a sexual exchange between them. Mama was a pretty woman, and she was kind to him, a kindness he obviously did not get from anyone else in his life. Moreover, he took extreme care not to cause her any problems with my stepfather. As a teenager, with a teenager's contempt for moral failings and sexual complexity of any kind, I had been convinced that Mama's relationship with that old man was contemptible. Also, that I would never do such a thing. But the first time a lover of mine gave me money and I took it, everything in my head shifted. The amount was not much to her, but it was a lot to me and I needed it. While I could not refuse it, I hated myself for taking it and I hated her for giving it. Worse, she had much less grace about my need than my mama's sugar daddy had displayed toward her. All that bitter contempt I felt for my needy cousins and aunts raged through me and burned out the love. I ended the relationship quickly, unable to forgive myself for selling what I believed should only be offered freely — not sex but love itself.

#

When the women in my family talked about how hard they worked, the men would spit to the side and shake their heads. Men took real jobs — harsh, dangerous, physically daunting work. They went to jail, not just the cold-eyed, careless boys who scared me with their brutal hands, but their gentler, softer brothers. It was another family thing, what people expected of my mama's people, mine. "His daddy's that one was sent off to jail in Georgia, and his uncle's another. Like as not, he's just the same," you'd hear people say of boys so young they still had their milk teeth. We were always driving down to the county farm to see somebody, some uncle, cousin, or nameless male relation. Shaven-headed, sullen, and stunned, they wept on Mama's shoulder or begged my aunt to help. "I didn't do nothing, Mama," they'd say, and it might have been true, but if even we didn't believe them, who would? No one told the truth, not even about how their lives were destroyed.

One of my favorite cousins went to jail when I was eight years old, for breaking into pay phones with another boy. The other boy was returned to the custody of his parents. My cousin was sent to the boys' facility at the county farm. After three months, my mama took us down there to visit, carrying a big basket of fried chicken, cold cornbread, and potato salad. Along with a hundred others we sat out on the lawn with my cousin and watched him eat like he hadn't had a full meal in the whole three months. I stared at his near-bald head and his ears marked with fine blue scars from the carelessly handled razor. People were laughing, music was playing, and a tall, lazy, uniformed man walked past us chewing on toothpicks and watching us all closely. My cousin kept his head down, his face hard with hatred, only looking back at the guard when he turned away.

"Sons-a-bitches," he whispered, and my mama shushed him. We all sat still when the guard turned back to us. There was a long moment of quiet, and then that man let his face relax into a big wide grin.

"Uh-huh," he said. That was all he said. Then he turned and walked away. None of us spoke. None of us ate. He went back inside soon after, and we left. When we got back to the car, my mama sat there for a while crying quietly. The next week my cousin was reported for fighting and had his stay extended by six months.

My cousin was fifteen. He never went back to school, and after jail he couldn't join the army. When he finally did come home we never talked, never had to. I knew without asking that the guard had had his little revenge, knew too that my cousin would break into another phone booth as soon as he could, but do it sober and not get caught. I knew without asking the source of his rage, the way he felt about clean, well-dressed, contemptuous people who looked at him like his life wasn't as important as a dog's. I knew because I felt it too. That guard had looked at me and Mama with the same expression he used on my cousin. We were trash. We were the ones they built the county farm to house and break. The boy who was sent home was the son of a deacon in the church, the man who managed the hardware store.

As much as I hated that man, and his boy, there was a way in which I also hated my cousin. He should have known better, I told myself, should have known the risk he ran. He should have been more careful. As I grew older and started living on my own, it was a litany I used against myself even more angrily than I used it against my cousin. I knew who I was, knew that the most important thing I had to do was protect myself and hide my despised identity, blend into the myth of both the good poor and the reasonable lesbian. When I became a feminist activist, that litany went on reverberating in my head, but by then it had become a groundnote, something so deep and omnipresent I no longer heard it, even when everything I did was set to its cadence.

#

By 1975 I was earning a meager living as a photographer's assistant in Tallahassee, Florida. But the real work of my life was my lesbian-feminist activism, the work I did with the local women's center and the committee to found a women's studies program at Florida State University. Part of my role, as I saw it, was to be a kind of evangelical lesbian feminist, and to help develop a political analysis of this woman-hating society. I did not talk about class, except to give lip service to how we all needed to think about it, the same way I thought we all needed to think about racism. I was a determined person, living in a lesbian collective — all of us young and white and serious — studying each new book that purported to address feminist issues, driven by what I saw as a need to revolutionize the world.

Years later it's difficult to convey just how reasonable my life seemed to me at that time. I was not flippant, not consciously condescending, not casual about how tough a struggle remaking social relations would be, but like so many women of my generation, I believed absolutely that I could make a difference with my life, and I was willing to give my life for the chance to make that difference. I expected hard times, long slow periods of self-sacrifice and grinding work, expected to be hated and attacked in public, to have to set aside personal desire, lovers, and family in order to be part of something greater and more important than my individual concerns. At the same time, I was working ferociously to take my desires, my sexuality, my needs as a woman and a lesbian more seriously. I believed I was making the personal political revolution with my life every moment, whether I was scrubbing the floor of the childcare center, setting up a new budget for the women's lecture series at the university, editing the local feminist magazine, or starting a women's bookstore. That I was constantly exhausted and had no health insurance, did hours of dreary unpaid work and still sneaked out of the collective to date butch women my housemates thought retrograde and sexist never interfered with my sense of total commitment to the feminist revolution. I was not living in a closet: I had compartmentalized my own mind to such an extent that I never questioned why I did what I did. And I never admitted what lay behind all my feminist convictions — a class constructed distrust of change, a secret fear that someday I would be found out for who I really was, found out and thrown out. If I had not been raised to give my life away, would I have made such an effective, self-sacrificing revolutionary?

The narrowly focused concentration of a revolutionary shifted only when I began to write again. The idea of writing stories seemed frivolous when there was so much work to be done, but everything changed when I found myself confronting emotions and ideas that could not be explained away or postponed until after the revolution. The way it happened was simple and unexpected. One week I was asked to speak to two completely different groups: an Episcopalian Sunday school class and a juvenile detention center. The Episcopalians were all white, well-dressed, highly articulate, nominally polite, and obsessed with getting me to tell them (without their having to ask directly) just what it was that two women did together in bed. The delinquents were all women, 80 percent Black and Hispanic, wearing green uniform dresses or blue jeans and workshirts, profane, rude, fearless, witty, and just as determined to get me to talk about what it was that two women did together in bed.

I tried to have fun with the Episcopalians, teasing them about their fears and insecurities, and being as bluntly honest as I could about my sexual practice. The Sunday school teacher, a man who had assured me of his liberal inclinations, kept blushing and stammering as the questions about my growing up and coming out became more detailed. I stepped out into the sunshine when the meeting was over, angry at the contemptuous attitude implied by all their questioning, and though I did not know why, so deeply depressed I couldn't even cry.

The delinquents were another story. Shameless, they had me blushing within the first few minutes, yelling out questions that were part curiosity and partly a way of boasting about what they already knew. "You butch or femme?" "You ever fuck boys?" "You ever want to?" "You want to have children?" "What's your girlfriend like?" I finally broke up when one very tall, confident girl leaned way over and called out, "Hey, girlfriend! I'm getting out of here next weekend. What you doing that night?" I laughed so hard I almost choked. I laughed until we were all howling and giggling together. Even getting frisked as I left didn't ruin my mood. I was still grinning when I climbed into the waterbed with my lover that night, grinning right up to the moment when she wrapped her arms around me and I burst into tears.

#

That night I understood, suddenly, everything that had happened to my cousins and me, understood it from a wholly new and agonizing perspective, one that made clear how brutal I had been to both my family and myself. I grasped all over again how we had been robbed and dismissed, and why I had worked so hard not to think about it. I had learned as a child that what could not be changed had to go unspoken, and worse, that those who cannot change their own lives have every reason to be ashamed of that fact and to hide it. I had accepted that shame and believed in it, but why? What had I or my cousins done to deserve the contempt directed at us? Why had I always believed us contemptible by nature? I wanted to talk to someone about all the things I was thinking that night, but I could not. Among the women I knew there was no one who would have understood what I was thinking, no other working-class woman in the women's collective where I was living. I began to suspect that we shared no common language to speak those bitter truths.

In the days that followed I found myself remembering that afternoon long ago at the country farm, that feeling of being the animal in the zoo, the thing looked at and laughed at and used by the real people who watched us. For all his liberal convictions, that Sunday school teacher had looked at me with the eyes of my cousin's long ago guard. I felt thrown back into my childhood, into all the fears I had tried to escape. Once again I felt myself at the mercy of the important people who knew how to dress and talk, and would always be given the benefit of the doubt, while my family and I would not.

I experienced an outrage so old I could not have traced all the ways it shaped my life. I realized again that some are given no quarter, no chance, that all their courage, humor, and love for each other is just a joke to the ones who make the rules, and I hated the rule-makers. Finally, I recognized that part of my grief came from the fact that I no longer knew who I was or where I belonged. I had run away from my family, refused to go home to visit, and tried in every way to make myself a new person. How could I be working class with a college degree? As a lesbian activist? I thought about the guards at the detention center. They had not stared at me with the same picture-window emptiness they turned on the girls who came to hear me, girls who were closer to the life I had been meant to live than I could bear to examine. The contempt in their eyes was contempt for me as a lesbian, different and the same, but still contempt.

While I raged, my girlfriend held me and comforted me and tried to get me to explain what was hurting me so bad, but I could not. She had told me so often about her awkward relationship with her own family, the father who ran his own business and still sent her checks every other month. She knew almost nothing about my family, only the jokes and careful stories I had given her. I felt so alone and at risk lying in her arms that I could not have explained anything at all. I thought about those girls in the detention center and the stories they told in brutal shorthand about their sisters, brothers, cousins, and lovers. I thought about their one-note references to those they had lost, never mentioning the loss of their own hopes, their own futures, the bent and painful shape of their lives when they would finally get free. Cried-out and dry-eyed, I lay watching my sleeping girlfriend and thinking about what I had not been able to say to her. After a few hours I got up and made some notes for a poem I wanted to write, a bare, painful litany of loss shaped as a conversation between two women, one who cannot understand the other, and one who cannot tell all she knows.

It took me a long time to take that poem from a raw lyric of outrage and grief to a piece of fiction that explained to me something I had never let myself see up close before — the whole process of running away, of closing up inside yourself, of hiding. It has taken me most of my life to understand that, to see how and why those of us who are born poor and different are so driven to give ourselves away or lose ourselves, but most of all, simply to disappear as the people we really are. By the time that poem became the story "River of Names,"[††] I had made the decision to reverse that process: to claim my family, my true history, and to tell the truth not only about who I was but about the temptation to lie.

#

By the time I taught myself the basics of storytelling on the page, I knew there was only one story that would haunt me until I understood how to tell it — the complicated, painful story of how my mama had, and had not, saved me as a girl. Writing *Bastard Out of Carolina*[†††] became, ultimately, the way to claim my family's pride and tragedy, and the embattled sexuality I had fashioned on a base of violence and abuse.

The compartmentalized life I had created burst open in the late 1970s after I began to write what I really thought about my family. I lost patience with my fear of what the women I worked with, mostly lesbians, thought of who I slept with and what we did together. When schisms developed within my community; when I was no longer able to hide within the regular dyke network; when I could not continue to justify my life by constant political activism or distract myself by sleeping around; when my sexual promiscuity, butch/femme orientation, and exploration of sadomasochistic sex became part of what was driving me out of my community of choice — I went home again. I went home to my mother and my sisters, to visit, talk, argue, and begin to understand.

Once home I saw that as far as my family was concerned, lesbians were lesbians whether they wore suitcoats or leather jackets. Moreover, in all that time when I had not made peace with myself, my family had managed to make a kind of peace with me. My girlfriends were treated like slightly odd versions of my sisters' husbands, while I was simply the daughter who had always been difficult but was still a part of their lives. The result was that I started trying to confront what had made me unable really to talk to my sisters for so many years. I discovered that they no longer knew who I was either, and it took time and lots of listening to each other to rediscover my sense of family, and my love for them.

It is only as the child of my class and my unique family background that I have been able to put together what is for me a meaningful politics, to regain a sense of why I believe in activism, why self revelation is so important for lesbians. There is no all-purpose feminist analysis that explains the complicated ways our sexuality and core identity are shaped, the way we see ourselves as parts of both our birth families and the extended family of friends and lovers we invariably create within the lesbian community. For me, the bottom line has simply become the need to resist that omnipresent fear, that urge to hide and disappear, to disguise my life, my desires, and the truth about how little any of us understand — even as we try to make the world a more just and human place. Most of all, I have tried to understand the politics of *they*, why human beings fear and stigmatize the different while secretly dreading that they might be one of the different themselves. Class, race, sexuality, gender — and all the other categories by which we categorize and dismiss each other — need to be excavated from the inside.

#

The horror of class stratification, racism, and prejudice is that some people begin to believe that the security of their families and communities depends on the oppression of others, that for some to have good lives there must be others whose lives are truncated and brutal. It is a belief that dominates this culture. It is what makes the poor whites of the South so determinedly racist and the middle class so contemptuous of the poor. It is a myth that allows some to imagine that they build their lives on the ruin of others, a secret core of shame for the middle class, a goad and a spur to the marginal working class, and cause enough for the homeless and poor to feel no constraints on hatred or violence. The power of the myth is made even more apparent when we examine how, within the lesbian and feminist communities where we have addressed considerable attention to the politics of marginalization, there is still so much exclusion and fear, so many of us who do not feel safe.

I grew up poor, hated, the victim of physical, emotional, and sexual violence, and I know that suffering does not ennoble. It destroys. To resist destruction, self-hatred, or lifelong hopelessness, we have to throw off the conditioning of being despised, the fear of becoming the they that is talked about so dismissively, to refuse lying myths and easy moralities, to see ourselves as human, flawed, and extraordinary. All of us — extraordinary.

---

† *A Few Words in the Mother Tongue: Poems, Selected and New,* Eighth Mountain Press: Portland, Oregon, 1990.
†† *Trash* (Firebrand Books: Ithaca, New York, 1988).
††† Dutton: New York, 1992.

Late Shift, The Davis Bee Biology Lab

Matt Yuranda

My hands do not sweat or shake,
but move with the lazy confidence of smoke
like my father taught me. It's 2 A.M.
and I pluck bees from the hive, stingers
prodding my thumbnail, and glue
small colored numbers to their abdomens,
and sometimes, I remember my father's combs
before dawn, the hours humming
with increments of bees,
and him saying
the hive is like a single animal,
gentle and hardworking, no meanness,
only plain simple reactions that give back
all the love, fear, and weakness
we bring to it, then catching my thin wrist,
ungloving my left hand, pressing it
to the comb until I calmed and my skin
cooled and the bees settled on my fingers
like snow.

At dawn, they drift off, and I watch Leon,
who moves like an astronaut in Thompson's field,
the white of his gloves and netted helmet
matching the rows of white hives.
Bees are his hobby, his solitude he says,
distance from the failed engines, the calibrations
and timings and tune-ups of the auto shop
which is his life.
On Tuesdays
and some Thursdays, we ride together
back to town before the town wakes, and I get out
at the library and walk the last mile,
street lights flickering off,
the smell of dew rising from lawns.

I know this path like a bee knows
the interjacence of its hive, the bee
who dances in its darkness of combs and remembers
its track through flowers by remembering the sun,
this path
through the auto yard,
inexhaustible cars giving themselves up,
the Buick on its chassis, early sun on chrome,
following the tailpipes and webs of glass
until I am climbing the iron staircase
that coils behind his apartment,

one more Tuesday steeped in a pattern
we've designed without words, not quite habit,
because habits are typical, thoughtless,
opening the door without knocking
and Leon stands the way he's always stood:
in his green shirt at the kitchen window,
holding the skillet that holds

his breakfast,
my dinner, and I am tired,
each Tuesday, and I lay down after our meal
under the east-facing window, the light
in his hair, starting and ending a day
with his slight weight and breath
like the sun slowly rising behind me.

Perhaps it is endurance, something we learn,
as my father says, without knowing
we are learning it, when I wake in darkness,
retrace the empty kitchen, cradling my shoes
on the iron staircase like a thief
who is certain he leaves no context,
nothing to follow or conclude,
and I am not afraid.
I am confident,
like my steady compilation of bees,
each night gentle, unhurried, the moon
not yet risen above the limitless Buick,
and not once do I hesitate, walking
through metal, rust, broken glass,
touching nothing.

Freeway

Tamar Perla

If he were to think of her here, now, he would begin to suffer, and he cannot stop to suffer, not here on the job. If he were to stop for a moment, stop the pounding, she would sink into the well of his stomach and pin him, impale him on her glistening girders and press the breath from his body with the ungiving crush of her concrete thighs. He is foolish to pretend that he isn't with her now, in the pounding that is for her, of her, his body vibrating with the smooth chopping of the metal drive into her concrete brick. He is worn with his feeling as the pile driver moves again and again between his feet in oily bootblack, he is tired of wanting and engaged to it, she weighing like a bomb against his neck. He shakes her off but she grows hands of sandpaper that rub him into smoke, hands of twisted steel that grope, lost, upon his rubber shelves, tearing his stacked organs into quivering shards. She grows hands and hands and hands, monstrous grasping deformity of love until he is shaking, useless, forgetting he is Foreman, wrecked with this work that is the dismembering of her, without which he is emptied even of the dead space in-between.

When he was — before he is now, when he was not crazy in love and mourning — he remembers quiet, how quiet it used to be. By the river he watched the swirling and eavesdropped on the conversing of blue-veined stones, leaves and water. Quiet talking, it wasn't his first language but his original voice and it eased his fire, when he needed it eased.

He doesn't understand it even now, after five months with her, five months since he started the job, tearing her down after the earthquake. At night he can't help himself, he climbs to her highest point and lays his body flat against her stretched, broken belly. She is so smooth and cool, hurting and distant, different now than when she swirled new and unborn, when she embraced him like a warm-limbed child with her raw, wet concrete. He had mixed her porridgy guts, reached his hand into the vat and pulled her gritty sinews between the fork of his fingers. He felt he was squeezing her heart, which moved against his hand with palpitations of love. Now lying flat against her he registers the small tremblings of the earth, of distant traffic, movements incidental to her inner vibration, to her deep heat that convects against his straining fingerpads, that bites at the heels of his hands with soft pricklings, a lover's tease. She is lightly powdered and this white dust marks his hands, his face, everywhere he touches her.

He is in love even with her death, with her dismembering, because of the life it raises in him. You used to roar, he laughs into her dust, to churn with the barrelwheeling combustibility of tooth-treaded rubber, sing with the balding tires' slap and spin, give to the weight of daddy loads of lumber, list and sigh and always hold. He is whispering to her now, his lips pressed softly to her oil-stained fleshrise, You are my girl, you are my best girl, you are my hard new baby and I must break you.

#

When the Foreman was a boy he held fear under his tongue like a big white pill. It'll choke me, it'll choke me, he told his stepfather, but the man was nearsighted and had to pull the boy closer to see what he was saying. That rough old thumb pushing down his throat, rubbing his front teeth and lips while the sour gin breath stank up his nose and curled wet and fleshy at the pink flower of his ear, It's good for you, son. When he cried the old man whipped him with a black-haired arm, Keeps us both strong. He was softer even than pretty Sue and liked to cross the street with her, holding her hand for safety, walking in step when the crossing guard signaled Go, arriving too quickly at the curb island where Sue turned right and he followed the hateful back alley home, Pretty Sue I love you don't turn away.

Once he grew hard the women found him and bent for him and wanted his life in return. He was married in a baffling ceremony that seemed to spin directly into the birth of his daughter. He sometimes had trouble remembering her face.

Love eluded him, days fell, murdered, the undead trees he had cleared from forests for years, acres of felled wisemen. Even in the quiet after-severing, howling spirits clawed his chest. He sat in broken branches and gathered his breath, wondering, was this what he was for? When he moved to construction he began to relax again. He didn't wake at night with the warm odor of pine still on his hands, rich under his fingernails, his lungs filled with its burning perfume, insistently alive. Instead he smelled of sweat and glue, varnish and lumber dust, silicone and tar and gravelsand. His wife said he smelled right but when he laid her down he felt he was burrowing in pine needles, buried in loam, panting with the worms and snails and creeping fibrous roots like a one-eyed-orificed creature trailing his path of slime, a slippery coil that reached before and beyond his crepuscular comprehension.

#

He doesn't know where they are now, wife and child, although they are probably where he left them when he crawled away from their crying. He tries to remember his life with the trees before he became their evergreen affliction. He has bred so much pain, so little love, and never thought to purchase mending tools; now is too late, he is a veteran of tearing down.

Sometimes he wishes for arms, to hold him, to reach toward, to fall into. He is ashamed, but she is so hard — until he feels her again, alive, her girdered spine twisting in his hands, his instrument, Oh play me, play me.

#

There is the woman who watches. She sees him climb the arched ramp, lie on his belly on a jagged extension and reach into the mangled spokes of metal to crumble cement between his fingers, sometimes place a piece in his mouth. She sees him move in a shadow of dust, gray mur-

mur against the smog-filtered sunset, and fall to the white line in a dance of yearning. She thinks she sees, in her isolation she thinks to save him, in her cage she straps herself tight with her love.

She has not left the house in weeks, this is one of the bad times but she will come through eventually — something always leads her out. Two times before it was a red-winged blackbird, drifted on the window sill, reminding her of the day and movement, sweet upon the wind. Last time it was cherry pie — so corny, she knows — but she smelled it from her childhood and had to have the canned cherries that she ate pawed into a soup bowl with her fingers, reliving the panic of searching grocery aisles, standing in line with her hands throbbing from holding the cans so tightly, trying to make herself look into the cashier's eyes like a normal person would, an out-and-about person running errands, a young woman baking some pies for a bake sale maybe, unable to get fresh cherries, her wild look reflected in the checkboy's eye. He was good-looking and the sweat ran hot down her sides, her body a ragged conductor of fear and self-conscious scent, sparks splitting the ends of her hair with sharp crackling pops. She was sure if anyone tried to touch her they would fry hard and shuddering.

At home she watches the man love the freeway and thinks, I have a love, too, reaches into the cupboard for a can of cherries, she keeps dozens now, may never have to go back to that store again, opens the can savagely. She crams cherries into her mouth and sucks them down without chewing, rubs them against her throat and belly and between her legs, crouches naked in the sticky filling and gags picturing the clotted red necks of toads, how they expand with air then pull back, her eyes level with their glassy sliding eyes, her rump in the mud with the tadpoles and fishes, slippery swimmers gliding over her buttocks and between, she sinking into the sucking mouths of mudholes and split by poking twigs that hide beneath the surface. I have a love, she spits up cherry dribble, clutches into a child-ball and lies quiet, perspiring in thin trickles down her branching spine, And he's a lot like you.

#

Sometimes the freeway talks to him as he sits in moonlight, back against her guardrail — at least the woman thinks she sees the talking, sees him nod and close his eyes as if to words. Alone with her hands deep in flowerpots of soil and water, squeezing the grainy gristly mud in angry fists that act on their own — her face smiling, calm, as her hands throw wet clumps of dirt against the walls. She cannot hear the conversation that is taking place, a monologue, actually, with perfectly timed pauses that allow him to act his part, receptacle. Are you sure you want this? Because you can't tell it, you will remain sheet faced; ours is an unspeakable association. Yes, he nods, I want the unspeakable. The freeway gives, suddenly, along a previously cracked leg. Dust rises as she crumbles slightly, pebbles kicking down the mountain of her, an exhalation of musty rot oozing from her side, an ill-winded humor seeping from her gangrenous limb where the early crew had hosed down a human campsite laid at her feet. I will choke you, she sputters, and he leans his head back to see how she looks upside-down, smog and gravel in somersault, his head wide open to its own interior sky, a child's plastic beachball with jumping bell inside. Choke me then. When the faint drift of his laughter reaches the woman she stops her necessary scrubbing of the window ledge to listen. It goes on and on, his laugh, deep-gutted and unafraid, and she watches him on his back moving his arms and legs like a child in the snow, or, an insect on its pin. Tomorrow, she speaks out loud to the window, her voice scratchy and hollow, high-pitched with disuse, scaring her so that she clears her throat and tries to hum lightheartedly, then repeats herself in a deep toady croak, Tomorrow I am going Out.

#

One day, the golden dream. The woman is out and about. The Foreman sits on a slab of metal that is pleasingly unrecognizable to her, unwraps a sandwich from the old-fashioned deli, the Dilly-Deli, that insists on waxed paper and fist-sized pickles. Months have passed and he is rebuilding. Soon the city's angels will be invited to return to their freeway perches. She is wearing a print dress, button-down, fluttery at the knee, open at the collar, porcelain blue flowers that make her eyes pop out. I've seen you, she says, Well, watched you really, from my apartment, it's across from the freeway. He winces slightly to hear her spoken of offhandedly, as if she's just what comes between apartments and people, but a Hollywood breeze blows up the woman's dress, she has conveniently unbuttoned the last six buttons and he sees her porcelain blue flowered panties reaching into a fetchingly plump cleft that angles from between her thighs with an almost beckoning thrust; if it were an eye, the heavily mascaraed lash would do its moth dance, if a hand, its red-lacquered finger would uncurl and curl voluptuously in his direction, but the sudden wind drops, her skirt falls back into chaste ripples and they find themselves eye-to-eye, never mind the pickle in his hand.

You are a handsome man, she says, A pity to waste when there are women starving uptown. I brought you some dessert. It's cherry pie and although he prefers banana cream she's flesh and blood, not concrete and steel, and he can tell she's pliant. I like a woman who wants what she gets, he tells her before setting their dinner date. Wear something tight and black and bring your credit card, go easy on the hair spray. She wants him to reach her inside out until she bleeds cherry filling, to keep her a prisoner chained to a metal link in the floor, he never copies the one key but keeps it dangling on a hook just out of her reach. They fall in love.

#

There is a freeway unlike any other. Beautifully composed, she denies her awkward buttresses, strains toward the greenish sky, is glorious in her man's fringy adoration. This metropolis is no place for fairy tales.

All he knows is the feel of her, the stretch of her, how he could make his bed in her, how she asks for nothing and everything, just in being loved and made of concrete. It will take more than a pair of flowered underpants to sway him from this devotion. She is the first girl who couldn't be hurt, who couldn't hurt back. For him the woman doesn't exist, has or has never left her room, sits or doesn't on the floor with a Slinky he can't see twisted up around both arms, wears or doesn't her exoskeleton like a carnival float; her hair floats only in the wind of her dream. He has never met her, she doesn't leave her house! Flaunting her, See I too have pretty metal tentacles, love me. Love me.

Oaths of Secrecy

Secret societies, most often composed of men, have existed in all cultures. Initiation brings with it the responsibility to keep the secrets of the group, with punishments defined for failure to do so. Consider these Chinese Triad oaths from about 1840:

If you debauch a brother's wife, daughter, or sister, you will perish under the knife.

If a brother becomes prosperous, you will not extort from him, and if you do, you will die by the sword.

Should you by mistake rob a brother of his property, you will restore it to him as soon as you find out that he is a brother. If you do not, may you vomit blood and die.

If you meet a brother fighting with another man, you shall inquire, and if he is in the right, you must help him. If he is in the wrong, you must dissuade him. You shall not assist another man and insult a brother, for if you do, may the god of the Thunder destroy you.

Four Secrets I Kept From Wife Life

Lidia Yuknavitch

ONE

You don't see radiators much anymore. They are old-fashioned, they are inside of old buildings. People have learned. Almost anyone knows not to lean on one. She lived in an old building, the kind with radiators. Up close, they seem like magnified bars. She took a deep breath. She touched her cheek to the radiator for three long seconds in a perfectly calm gesture, a kind of uninspired gesture, but deliberate all the same. "One, two, three…" she said, letting the air out of her mouth with each word. One, two, three; the heat singed silent and deep through the layers of her skin, through the fleshy part of her cheek.

What patience. What brave, glorious, undaunted patience. When she had finally thought of it, how proud at her own intellect she had been. And even then she had realized it would take patience — patience to sit in front of the hot metal, patience to draw her face near, and nearer even as the heat became evident, whispering toward her cheek. Patience at the moment itself, so as to do it right, to pull away slowly, because she did not, after all, want to rip half of her face off and leave it staring back at her from the radiator. She wanted a controlled effort, a specific result. Only a wound, a perfect wound. She was absolutely confident at the idea of it, because what was this patience compared to her life? Three small seconds.

#

The first thing she did was pour herself a glass of whiskey. A glass one might fill with milk. She drank it down until the heat in her throat and chest challenged the fire in her right cheek, the fire filling up the whole right side of her face now, making her nostril flare a little, her lip quiver, her eye close. The whiskey streamed down the center of her body — high voltage.

She thought of things her women friends said to her. Advice, consolations over scripted lunches. Come on, be serious, get a grip. You don't really hate him, do you? How cliché. For Christ's sake grow up, be sensible, have a little self-control. Go on a diet — herbs and tofu. Change your hair. Your wardrobe. Your perfume. Your heels. Make something of your life. Sex isn't everything, don't be ridiculous. You are obsessing. You are playing the victim. You are just being lazy. I wish *I* had your problem. Or her personal favorite, Honey, what you need is a good fuck.

How do you tell women who wear false nails and baby powder between their legs and order chicken salads with vinaigrette dressing at linen-covered tables and who are busy trying desperately to chew without smudging lipstick that women must keep moving or die?

She walked around her living room holding her drink, feeling animated. Alive. Gesturing with her drink to the TV, the couch, the different objects in the room, speaking aloud from time to time. What advice, she wanted to know, was there for epic anger and hate equaled only in intensity by need? She bent to confront the end table. "Have you guessed at my sense of desperation? Where should I put my anger? Who can my anger take care of? Make love to? Where does a woman put her anger? In marriage? In children? Lovers? Contact sports? Alcohol, drugs, violence? Because buddy," and here she took a step back from the end table for effect, "we're not just talking about the kind of anger you can bake away or submerge in dishwater or paint with red lips or do lunch over or cover over with some Victoria's Secret silky little treasure…I'm *pissed*…I mean,

69

I am fucking pissed off…" She paused. She looked seriously at the end table. "Well?" No one answered, the room swelled with shame, silence, and ignorance.

The now cold pain in her cheek pierced all the way through her skull. She thought maybe her right eye had swollen shut; anyway, she could no longer open it. She went to the bathroom to have a look. On her way she realized this was all a little disgusting, a little over dramatic, a little raw. She realized if she were to tell someone about it, they might just as soon not order anything to eat, they might lean a little away from her in the listening. They would really rather not, not in public, not so close. She whispered to the bathroom door before she opened it, "Should we keep quiet?" She opened the door, looked herself in the face.

Hey! It really was a beauty! She examined it: the outer edge was deep red and crimped, then a kind of purplish welt rising on either side like mangled lips. In the center of that a pussy, long, yellowish bubble of blistered skin oozing and retreating like sea foam. An amazing wound. A well thought out, a carefully executed wound. The perfect. The living end.

By the time he got home, she'd be out already. By the time he got home, she'd have outlined her own eyes in black, blue lashes. By the time he got home, she'd be blushed and lipsticked — what else, red as a Coca-Cola can. By the time he got home — after she'd stared at the tools of the face for a long while — she'd have decided on a gold dust shadow, she'd have traced a glow around the thing, precious metal. By the time he got home, she'd be sitting in a bar with the most perfect wound imaginable. There'd be no way to miss it.

TWO

Goddamn it to mother-fucking hell, she says.

I'd say that just about covers it, he says. He wants to know why she feels the need to swear so much, so deliberately, what depends on it and why is it so important. Why for so long she hasn't grown tired. Worn-out in the mouth. As he says this he rubs the back of his long neck with long-fingered hands of grace. He thinks of a painting of a woman who is only mouth. Any mouth but hers. He has everything to say but rarely speaks. She looks straight into his eyes, straight into his skull, says fuck you. It's curious, he says, curious because now when she uses profanity it sounds like everyone else's ordinary speech. Like when she says goddamn it she may as well be saying the kettle is steaming. She would not say that she is angry but her eyes flash hard at him saying this to her, as if her language did not disrupt, did not slice open the air and slash him across his goddamned stupid too-beautiful face. She knows he is lying. What really is curious is that these two are lovers. This is love. The reason she is swearing is because they are on their way to an evening party. He knows what she means. The parties they attend together are full of falseness. Because he is an artist in San Francisco. There is nothing real about artists in San Francisco, not the art, not the women who live with them, not the galleries, not the critics, not the men who live with them, not even San Francisco — everything is filmy, filmy as bay fog. Except maybe for their hands. The hands are priceless.

All of them together make one big pile of shit she declares grabbing hold of his hand as they approach the door of the evening party. He squeezes her hand. She squeezes back thinking how meaningless, wondering where is the risk in squeezing a lover's hand while walking to an evening party?

They pass rows of colored houses remarking at the features like so many faces. Her descriptions: the fucking amazing view, the goddamn little rows of windows stretching for fucking miles. His: more azure evening light, warm glow from the inside out, houses alive. Doors, windows, roofs speaking. They make a good pair, or rather, their mouths make a good pair — hers pushing out, exploding, his soaking everything in slow and sweet.

Near the house they will enter she suggests wildly why don't they run back down the hill, past the houses again, past the doors and windows and faces into only the evening. She unbuttons her blouse. He can barely see her, the light is dim. She tugs at his arm and he half believes her, as always. But they do enter the house because someone sees him and calls out his name. She leaves her excitement standing in the yard, leaning in the direction of the night, eyes wide, chest heaving, naked.

Inside everyone calls him Pater. His name is Peter she keeps reminding them, but she is the only one who calls him this. Finally some man with mostly a bald head except for some gray on the sides that he has had styled and sculpted explains to her that Pater sounds more like the name of an artist — that more people will buy from a Pater than a Peter. She is astounded that he thinks he must tell her this. The paintings: what is being bought? Sometimes she can't remember his name at all, simply his painting. There are a lot of drinks. Language in the rooms of the party suddenly turns liquid. Animals begin crawling out. One man becomes a lizard, his belly scraping the shag carpet, his arms and legs sticking out stiff from his body. Another man who has been pinching the asses of women all night turns into a crab, with one, huge, red, heavy claw, so heavy he cannot lift it anymore. A woman with big lips becomes a blowfish, bubbles rise from her face now and then, her eyes move to the sides of her head and look magnified. Pater or Peter becomes a bird with heavy, colored plumage, terribly magnificent. His back sways, his chest protrudes.

She drinks scotch continually. She still feels like a fucking person. She goes into the bathroom and removes her bra and underwear from underneath her clothing and stuffs them into the medicine cabinet. She emerges from the bathroom some new animal no one has ever seen before. Everyone notices her. She names herself something between the color red and the word devour. She looks for him.

Some small man who might be a ferret or a weasel is talking to Pater/Peter, the rooster or the peacock. Everything swims. She watches her lover shrink. She moves closer. The ferret/weasel's mouth is making sharp, jerky movements. Closer still she hears words like ridiculous and no talent and not a chance in hell. Her lover is shrinking before the weasel into a small bird, then into a chick, peeping uselessly. The ferret-man's tongue looks long and dangerous, his lips are knives moving together, slicing and clicking.

She hates. She hates the ferret, she hates the smallness of the chick. She hates the alcohol, she hates the party, the animals, the body who came into the house. The ferret's mouth becomes the only thing she can focus on, even as a crowd is gathering because by now of course she has started swearing, even as the fish-woman swims up and blows diplomatic bubbles between them, even as the giant red pincher drags itself near, the ferret's mouth clicks and slices and becomes more clear than is possible, so that finally she has a direction for her hate to aim at, and she punches his mouth right off his face. Everyone is a person again, humanly stunned.

A man rests on the floor. Her knuckles ache. Some quiet hands lead her away, a man whose name she cannot remember. He is saying it's alight, it's alight. She suddenly realizes this is how she feels every goddamn night of her fucking life. His hands are on her face, her shoulders, he tries to sculpt her OK. Her own hands hang useless.

This love cannot live unless she fights him every day of her life. He paints, will paint. She aches for the years, the marriage, the waiting to be over, to summer over into a different life. She runs toward summer with no hands. He will paint with or without her.

THREE

Truth is, I don't like to talk first or drink wine or pretend there is something significant that can occur in the space of time before fucking a woman. But I usually do a lot of talking, drinking wine, seeing films, and discussing moral issues in an intelligent and meaningful way before the bedroom. See, what I would really prefer is to get them down on the floor, get in them and watch their faces reveal just how much they can't live without it, how they might die if they couldn't have it. I would like to finger their nipples hard, I would like them to say fuck me again and again. But the thing is, I am thirty-five and successful and well educated and civilized and even that thing women demand these days, sensitive. So I treat them with respect, as an equal, while at the same time adoring them, because of course you can't leave out adoring them — then they wouldn't be the kind of equal they want.

Last night I was at a movie, a German movie, or film, with an intellectual audience: lots of black clothing and designer glasses and shoes with exotic names. A blonde woman sat down next to me after the film started. I looked at her. She looked at me. There were maybe twenty other people there in the dark. Do you want to fuck me? she whispers, as if she has just said, excuse me but do you have the time. Same quizzical look as, do I know what time it is.

I know, I couldn't believe it either. I'm not sure what to say, I mean, on the one hand, here she is, the woman I dream of saying fuck me in just the right tone, the answer to my prayers, no small talk, no seduction, no familiarity. She doesn't know that I am successful, sensitive, and civilized. She doesn't care.

But on the other hand, she could be crazy, all that disease out there right now, or perhaps pregnant and ready to claim paternity later, or even worse, a man dressed as a woman…I saw a movie like that. But then she slid from her seat onto the floor and spread out down there where you usually see old popcorn glowing in the dark and your feet stick a little. She unbuttons her blouse and two luminous globes. She unzips her jeans and I smell gold like hay. I try to watch the movie and her at the same time but eyes were not made to look up and down simultaneously. And she pulled me by the eyeballs down on to her.

I'm thirty-five years old. I'm at this goddamn German movie alone because the woman who was supposed to meet me canceled. A young flip thing. Canceled dinner, canceled the movie, the talk, the wine, the sex. I have a headache in my pelvis. And now I am on the floor, not wondering about disease or paternity but will we be heard. I hold my breath, move in her using only the muscles of my belly. Something German speaks to us.

Suddenly she is on top. I am pinned. I hold my wrists over my head. I imagine the whole thing in a movie. Her hair hangs down in my face. I am still trying to figure out how she got on top and if I care when I realize she is sitting straight up now, riding me for all she is worth. My penis is screaming but my brain is terrified of being seen. I begin to fear an usher-police figure. I try to pull her by the hair back down, out of view, but she won't have it. Now she is arching, her neck and hair make a silhouette against the glow of light which is the film, the film, my god. I reach for her nipples but she slaps my hand away, fingers her own nipples. I wonder if she has drawn the audience away from the film.

I feel it welling up in my thighs. I feel it prickle the surface of my skin. I feel it being sucked out of my body. She wants it so bad, I'm going to give it to her. I close my eyes, dig my fingers into her ass, feel the shiver of the body overtaking the brain. It's coming…it's coming….

Then she stops. I almost yell goddamn it, don't stop, for Christ's sake don't stop, you can't stop now, but the Germans are yelling already, and she has turned to watch. I hear some kind of brawl accompanying my torment, slapping and screams and chairs being thrown. I hear it is a woman screaming, a man slapping. I tug at her hips because I think I may explode from the inside out if she doesn't move again soon. Just ten seconds more. Please, just ten more seconds. I shake her from the waist. Her wet wiggles a bit. I get that pain in my temple and throat I got when I tried not to cry as a kid, only worse. Please, I beg. I grab my penis because I can't stand it anymore. I come like an ocean, a hydrant, a whale, ridiculous, I bite the inside of my cheek to keep quiet. When I open my eyes she is dressed, she is sitting in her seat, eyes forward, having slid off of me long ago. I am the sticky on the floor at her feet.

My rage is all whisper: how could you do that to me? Are you some kind of weirdo? Who the hell do you think you are? How could you do that? Are you psycho? Some loony? She doesn't whisper, though she speaks in a low voice.

You actually think I did it for you? Why, I don't even know you.

I must have seen over fifty foreign films that year.

FOUR

How'd you get the name Eddie?

Father gave it to me. Edwina.

I like the way she wants to watch, to see what's going on, even if she doesn't get it. I mean, when she came in to the garage, she tells me, the car makes a strange sound when I shift the gears. What kind of sound. This is usually where people make asses of themselves. They try to sound like a sick motor. But she says, you know that noise you hear when your alarm goes off in the morning, only you're not awake yet so you don't exactly hear it, you sense it, something between a buzz and a ring, and for a moment you don't know if it's a hangover or a dream or the phone or the alarm or an insect or a snore? I had to admit I knew what she meant. I overslept a lot. Didn't help me worth a shit to guess what was wrong with the car, but it did make me curious. She knew what she was talking about even though she didn't.

So when she came over to where I was under the hood, I said, could you hand me that Allen. She picked the tool up and looked at it a long time before she handed it to me. She got some oil on her hand, and she looked at that too.

I worked on her car. She stayed very near. So, she says, how long did it take you to learn to be a mechanic? Now she is making circles with her ring finger in a blob of oil near the battery. She's leaning right under the hood with me.

Better watch all that hair. I picked it up real fast. Think I had a knack for it. I've been around a garage all my life, it seemed natural. The oil, the smell of gasoline, the chrome, the black innards of an engine. I was helping with the repair work by the time I was twelve.

Now she is fingering the tools. She's asking me their names, what they are used for. It is the kind of conversation that makes you feel good about what you know.

I kind of start enjoying the company. I mean, I still think she is a little weird, like when she starts asking me about the engine parts. She says, Don't you think they are a lot like body parts, like that tube over there that curls underneath that other thing looks like a penis, and that thick curved thing like an arm with a flexed muscle, that big thing in the middle with all the compartments could be the lungs, it even looks like it's meant for air, and all of it together here under the hood, and us inside it tightening and screwing and greasing. Now all this not only sounds weird, but it starts sounding like sex.

So now we're both oily and curious, I guess.

When you were little, did your dad teach you things? You know, like how to throw a baseball?

Not really. Just mechanics. He was real busy. What about you? You look athletic. Big!

I was very good at sports. Better than the boys.

Good for you.

I guess I was a tomboy. I didn't have many girl friends. Except for two. One was a cheerleader. The other was one that nobody else talked to. She had red hair and glasses. She used to sit in those cement tunnels all through recess. One time I went in there, just to see if she really was a spastic like everyone said. I sat in there with her. I said, is your mamma spastic too like everyone says? And she lifted up her skirt and I thought I saw a peach between her legs. She petted herself and I could see the little hairs were reddish. And she said, see this? This is very rare. I was scared, but I believed her, because when I got home I couldn't find any hairs. I didn't think she was spastic anymore and I went in the tunnel more after that.

Pretty weird stuff. I just keep working even though by now I'm getting horny, I don't know, I guess it's the weirdness. Everybody gets excited by things that scare them a little. Not that she scared me, not really, except that now I notice that she is holding the biggest tool of all and swinging it a bit. I've read stories, you know? Women are doing strange things these days. I think, don't be silly, don't be so paranoid. She's weird, not crazy.

Then she says the weirdest thing of all, what do you think about pain, just out of the blue.

I play it real cool. Don't like it, I say.

Not even a little? Like when you get a backrub and they hit a muscle that is very sore and it hurts how they rub but you just can't get enough — what about that?

Well, I guess everybody likes that.

And what about fear?

Now the tools are a little slippery in my hands and I start sizing her up, thinking if that arm raises even a little I'll swing this Allen around into her stomach, just hurt her enough to scare her, because after all I really am bigger than her and could pin her to the garage floor easily. But the second I imagine her really trying to hit me, I realize that I am wet and throbbing and she is just setting the tool back down like the most normal person in the entire universe.

You little tease, I think, but what I come up with after all this is that I want to take her home and it makes me feel like somebody besides myself. And I think, is this how it feels?

I bet she busts a lot of balls.

Open and Shut

Elizabeth Hurst

Listen to me before you
open your mouth and thrust
your moist secrets into
another stranger's hands.

The soft sea-self you found
at that padded clinic swelled
fat and glassy as a tide pool
as the soured years slid out
from behind your teeth. The
hydra-headed oracle across
from you priced your pain
and polished it until it was
interesting enough to share —
and you walked away from

that office door, drunk on
splayed self and eager for
the husband and mother
you taught yourself to see
in every stranger's face.
But out here, among unpaid
ears and consuming lives,
we carry our seas inside.

Pull in your soul's membranes;
close your mouth before the sun
eats the shine off your tongue.
Banish yourself from that
shrinking paradise, and let
the world's predatory light
rest on those clean tools
of intelligent love locked
inside your public heart.

Guarding the Word

Toni Kennedy

Over the years faithful letter writers learn to deceive by honing the vice of restraint. They resist the intimate phrase, the forbidden word. Recently I reread the letters that I wrote to my parents when I was a Franciscan nun. I combed these documents for a bit of sadness or a snippet of humor, some insights that revealed how I had grown wiser. The shallowness of my communication saddened me. The words bloomed like too many pansies in a garden, concentrated color that would not endure through autumn. So many pieces of paper sent home between 1961 and 1984. So much history not shared. Why would anyone want to hold on to these letters, I asked myself and railed against my mother's decision to keep such insignificant records. Later I reflected upon the possibility that deceit is part of mail: postcards with too little space, sweepstakes envelopes with too many capitalized promises, electronic messages too accessible and letters with words too carefully chosen. Selective dishonesty is part of on-going communication.

In *The Pickwick Papers* Charles Dickens devotes a chapter to the art of letter-writing. One of his characters, Sam Weller, has just completed a lengthy valentine to his beloved Mary, and when his father appears, Sam reads the manuscript aloud. The father responds in Dickens' inimitable style.

"That's rather a sudden pull up, ain't it, Sammy?" inquired Mr. Weller.

"Not a bit on it," said Sam. "She'll vish there wos more, and that's the great art of letter writing."

The unpenned line and the emotion that never quite breaks the surface keep old women and love-struck soldiers waiting for the mail to arrive. The fine art of letter writing does not demand full disclosure. The writer willfully restrains herself. By what she leaves out, she teases the reader and leaves him wishing for more.

Pickwick's Sam and nuns in the cloister used the same phrase to describe what matters most. Desire for "the more" was how post-Vatican II theologians defined religious life. Everything about the food we ate, the cells where we slept, the feelings we expressed and the letters we wrote reflected the hidden life and the quest for "the more." This relinquishment of the natural in exchange for the supernatural gives birth to asceticism, but denial can give rise to concealment and concealment to deceit.

In the convent as I knew it, restraint and sacrifice were the heartbeats uniting sisters past, present and to come. Acts repeated generation after generation linked memories that came to have a life all their own. Ritual kept these memories pulsing. In the novitiate, that splendid mix of the contemplative life and bootcamp, letter-writing continued the order's tradition, for what the members chose to write about declared publicly who this Franciscan community was. Once a month we gathered in the community room, a wide, airy space of windows, green linoleum, straight-backed chairs and long wooden tables. The twenty of us understood the utter clarity of our purpose: to write one inspirational letter to our parents; no quick note to friends; no tangential correspondence to grandparents or siblings. True to the sisters who had come before us and would come after us, we sat in silence, sifting through events, collecting only the edifying ones.

When I read of Sam's inkstand and gilt-edged paper, the hard-nibbed pen; how he dusts the table, removes all crumbs from the surface, tucks up his sleeves, squares his shoulders and composes himself to write, I relive the preparation for correspondence. Is this where both restraint and deceit intersect? I see myself as I once was, with my wrist in Palmer position, aiming the end of the pen toward my right shoulder, listening to Smetana's *Moldau*.

The ritual associated with preparation is not unique to those long-ago convent days. A friend of mine mentioned that he had just purchased an eighty-dollar pen, and thus had pledged to become a letter writer. Another friend shops for the crafted card and then files each according to type: thank-you, sympathy, birthday, shower, anniversary. In lamp light over the left shoulder, with pen and paper, or the aptly named WordPerfect software program, will words come magically? It is as if the preparation accomplished the act of writing.

In the novitiate, on those Sunday afternoons, we could procrastinate for only so long. Our task was to produce a letter. The letter never served as just a message between the young nun and her parents. Her words were meant for a wider audience; meant to portray the bliss of turning one's back on the world. The novice mistress read every letter we wrote and every letter sent to us. Felony had no meaning in the convent.

Once someone said to me, "How violated you must have felt!" I try to recall my resentment, but simply remember my decision to be careful. I had entered a community whose traditions had survived any one nun's feeling of offense. The bumper sticker "Question Authority" would not have been found on convent cars in those days. This institution, like all institutions, did not exist for the purpose of humor or continual self-analysis. The Catholic church did not establish the Sisters of St. Francis as a gathering for diversity, but as a stable, rooted community, an alternative to a society continually in flux. Until I professed my final vows nine years later, I knew my written words reached beyond me. Free of mistakes, flawlessly penned, the letters reflected not only upon me, but upon the entire order. I chose to continue the tradition. Willingly I forgot the taste of envelope glue or the excitement of opening my own mail.

Ideally, letters are a living testament to our interests, education, sensibilities, disillusionments, and ecstasies: the real us, laid bare. Sam Weller smeared out wrong letters with his little finger and retraced the new letters so that they were visible through the blots. Few of us wish to be so revelatory. We destroy correspondence with too many mistakes; we type on letterhead to give credence to our words; we pass the document through spell-check. We write generic holiday letters that inform joyfully and that offend no relative's sensibilities. Instinctively we suspect that our letters might find a broader reading and we want any extended audience sympathetic and appreciative. We hope that our words will live beyond us, generation after generation: intact, unshredded, unrecycled, becoming part of the world's ancient tradition. Perhaps there is a novice mistress in all of us.

The art of correspondence, as Dickens' Weller declares, is not to tell all. In those early years as a nun, I did find it difficult to proclaim eternally God's blessings; to pull from my weary mind the utter joy of rising at five A.M. Now, when I read aloud the letters, I try to hear my words as my parents would have heard them twenty or thirty years ago. Such upbeat documents, replete with adjectives, restrained in matters of the heart. In hindsight, I wonder what fissure in the enclosure walls would have opened if I had described the weekly bite of the small whip called "the discipline." Would the glass covering the portraits of the Mother Superiors have cracked if I had questioned archaic practices like kissing the floor or begging a penance for a broken cup? Now I seek the human in these documents. I wish my mother could have laughed over the cook who had too many grapes one season and created new and nauseous recipes; the worst of which was to plant them like purple land mines in the chocolate pudding. Where were references to detestable Monday when we sweated over the clang, the splash, the hiss of machines? All I can find is references lauding the virtues of *labora* and daphne rising like cologne on the cloister walk.

Are such omissions so foreign in the world outside convent walls? I believe I join the long line of those who live in cloisters and those who amble in the marketplace. Guardians, all of us; one of a kind. Before home videos proved lucrative, families did not communicate in public form about their foibles. There was a prudence, a discretion concerning matters close to home. As the years in the convent passed and our ways became open to others, my writing habits did not change. My family never knew my struggles with obedience, my inability to adjust, or my homesickness. My parents entered, so it seemed, quite naturally into a similar deceit. They did not darken their letters with financial loss, fears for the future or their aching desire to have me come home. We wrote just enough to keep some parts of our lives a mystery. We wrote just enough to keep one another hungry for the mail.

Complete revelation is for the young, not the wise. Steve Duin, a newspaper columnist for the Portland *Oregonian* wrote about his youthful days when he "soaked page after page with the sap" of his life. He remembered "the shape of the word love on a piece of paper, the shudder of emotions that you couldn't trust to your tongue, only to your fingertips." Lack of guile is not the mark of the lifelong letter writer. No writer can afford such transparency, because what remains of us for the next encounter with inkstand and dusted table?

Mother's Day on Bushwick Ave.

Rick Rubin

I am not ashamed that I closed my hand around the wad of paper in darkest Brooklyn, beneath the elevated train lines. I did it because I felt life required it and recall it with a silent chuckle. Only the failure of the novel I wrote with the typewriter I bought with the wad of paper still rankles. Unpublished novels are heavy as stillborn babies. As for blame or shame or harm I may have caused, I admit nothing.

Brooklyn had an air of unreality for me. I am of Oregon, from which I run away sometimes, but always return. Brooklyn was the obverse of home, an obscured mirror image, white turned black, down become up. But having lost my most beloved, and finished a piece of writing, I'd run away from home, headed I thought for a Caribbean island.

Instead I found myself nearly broke in another kind of archipelago, a churning, grinding metropolis. I took the work I found: Caseworker 1 for the Department of Social Services of the City of New York. Any college graduate whatever his major could fight the war on poverty for D.S.S. of N.Y.C. that year.

Was I a good social worker? That would depend on your viewpoint. My supervisors were carefully noncommittal, but there were clerks who dreaded my coming, for the clients I served were waiting, and I wanted that grant now — Right Now! But of the 89 caseworkers who serviced the Williamsburg district of Brooklyn from Welfare Center 84, I alone was invited by the clients group to their Mothers Day party. I take some pride in that. It was from the Mothers Day party that the path branched off.

Bushwick Ave. twists south and then southwest through Williamsburg like the wagon road it probably originally was. It is broad and may have once been prosperous. Now there are four and five story brick tenements, vacant lots deep in rubbish, a few shops, crowds of people on stoops and sidewalks. The intersection of Melrose and Broadway was my idea of a true great cityscape. As if Franz Kafka had made it up and Hieronymus Bosch illustrated it. The Myrtle Avenue train piled on top of the Broadway line, both held up on black steel girders above cheap clothing and variety stores, pushcarts, and clamor. Squalid desperation to my innocent West Coast eyes. One time I saw a woman with a machete and fierce mad eyes rushing down the street. People got out of her way, but nobody took much interest. There was a diner where I used to go just to watch the fastest sandwich-maker on earth. God, that man could move his hands. It sure wasn't a slum for lack of trying. Just the wrong end of Long Island.

On Bushwick Ave. was a storefront office called Community Action Center #5, meant to aid the suffering denizens. Funded separately, the C.A.C. was in perpetual stormy opposition to the welfare department, as it was meant to be. Between, like gravel between millstones, we caseworkers were ground fine. Other caseworkers avoided the C.A.C. like a disease. Only I visited it. I got to know some of the workers there. They weren't my enemies; after all, we had the same clients. Maybe they could help me. At least I thought I ought to stay in touch. There I met Hosea Pendleton, a local Brooklyn guy, a burly black ex-Army military policeman in charge of housing problems. Hosea and I got to be pretty good friends. We'd saunter out for a beer sometimes, comparing notes on the situation.

I remember thinking it was swell when Hosea told me he planned to buy a car and take his wife for a vacation in Mexico. From my

West Coast standpoint, Mexico wasn't all that exotic. T-town was just across the border, Ensenada not far beyond. And everyone had a car, didn't they? Not me, for I was saving up to get out of New York City as soon as I could. But almost everyone else. A car was certainly not beyond the realm of possibility. Of course, Hosea was talking a swift, stylish car, but what did I know about his finances, or how old the car was?

I was pleased when the clients' group invited me to the Mothers Day party. My client, Mrs. Rodriquez, was president. I hadn't gotten to know Mrs. Rodriquez very well, because she spoke almost no English, and my survival Spanish, good enough in Mexico, made sense of hardly a tenth of the words in Puerto Rican. Puerto Rican seemed a language as guttural as German and shorn of suffixes like Neapolitan Italian, its idioms incomprehensible to my high school Castilian ear. I soon gave up and communicated to my ladies in welfare pidgin English.

Since I gave Mrs. Rodriquez, like all my other 60 "wives," every dollar allowed, I was not merely liked but well liked, and invited to the party. My 60 (mostly Puerto Rican) wives? Weren't they wives, in every sense but the carnal? And Serafina Diaz was even...ah, but Mrs. Diaz is another story. I came by and looked at receipts to see that they were paying the rent and utilities, checked report cards and argued about how they were raising the kids. I refurbished their wardrobes twice a year, issued special grants for school clothes, gave them new furniture when needed, or permission to move if the place was too hideous. So I didn't have sex with them, so what? A lot of husbands don't have sex with their wives. As for all those special grants for clothes and furniture, why not? They were greatly underfunded. I constituted myself a temporary ray of sunshine in their cloudy transplanted lives. I often wondered why they'd left that tropical island for this blustery northern one.

I'd decided after a few months that welfare was New York City's way of transferring the cost of keeping wages low to the federal government. The manufacturers hadn't upgraded their machinery, so they needed cheap labor, and the pool of wives and mothers being supported by welfare was a way of keeping their husbands or lovers content to work for minimum wages. The government was throwing money at poverty in 1968. I tried to throw as much as anyone.

The party was beer and eats in the crepe-paper decorated back room of C. A. C. #5; mothers and kids attended, but there was hardly a man in sight. It was no place for hanky-panky, so Hosea Pendleton and I ended up off in a corner. I brought up the name of one of the neighborhood landlords, Manny Klein, mentioning that a client of mine lived in one of Manny's rat-traps, and I planned to really go after the creep for refusing to fix numerous housing code violations. I asked for Hosea's advice about how to put the boots to that son-of-a-bitch slumlord.

Hosea started talking about how my client — a skinny, pale-black, gray-haired woman named Dorathea Winslow — was a nut case and that she was really troubling Manny Klein. Said she wouldn't pay her rent, and had her relatives break up the place. Hosea confided that in his opinion it wasn't entirely Klein's fault. I ought to see the owner's side too. Klein had tried to fix the place up, but the only tenants he could get were psychotics or Dorathea's relations — same thing — and no sooner had he fixed the lock on the door and replastered the walls than they busted everything all to hell again.

There was a ring of truth to that. As client, Dorathea left much to be desired. I'd visited her several times, trying to get her complaints straightened out. She was hard of hearing and harder still to deal with. Could talk, but would not listen.

It really was a hellish building. It's a crime people have to live in some of those buildings, but for reasons I could not fathom, more people wanted to live in the borough than there were places. The front door was permanently busted and the walls had gaping holes. Dangling lights, broken windows, dead rats. The trains clanged and rattled past a few feet away, the tenants hid behind their triple-locked doors. I'd knock and knock but Mrs. Winslow wouldn't answer. No way to reach her on the phone, but she could call me any time she wanted. When she did answer my knocking she filled my ear with rage. "I am Virgin Islands lady of good character much beset by travail, suh. Me trying to be proper lady but the landlord will fix nothing, so I will not pay him, for I am Virgin Islands lady of good... "

I accompanied her to court once. We met with the landlord's lawyer, a rumpled, hatchet-faced white with a pencil mustache. Suddenly she could hear a whole lot better. Standing outside the courtroom in a round classic-pillared marble rotunda loud with discordant babble, she and the attorney enacted an animated conversation. People, I supposed, could hear things at some decibel levels they couldn't hear at others. Or maybe she was reading his lips. They argued furiously, jigsawing out some sort of agreement; Klein was to fix this and that and she was to pay him portions of the rent. Never did go into the courtroom.

I felt something had been accomplished, and hoped it would work out so I never heard from her again. I didn't offer to send her special grants for clothes and furniture. Mrs. Winslow didn't seem like one of my wives. She was from a different Caribbean island entirely. But the apparent agreement didn't keep her from calling me again and again. Finally I sent her the special grants.

"Manny really wants to talk to you about that client of yours," Hosea told me, off to the side of the Mothers' Day party, talking fast but not too loud. "You really ought to hear his side of the story before you move on him. Lemme take you down to talk to him, okay man?"

Boy, was I dense. But finally, even I caught on. The car, the trip to Mexico, and now I ought to hear Klein's side of the story. My pal Hosea was on the take. It was a surprise, and kind of exciting. I'd never actually known anyone who took bribes.

East Coast people may find it hard to believe, but not much of that sort of thing goes on out in Oregon. Building inspectors just inspect buildings. That doesn't make them any easier to deal with, because the code is still the code. There are some lousy landlords, but they seldom offer to spread the wealth around. We like it that way, too. At least I do. But, what the hell, it was Brooklyn I was learning about. Or from. A giddy laugh nudged at my throat. "Okay," I told Hosea, "I'll talk to the man." Moments later we were hurrying down Bushwick Ave. toward Manny Klein's plumbing shop.

Klein's shop was a little hole in the wall with ducts, pipes, and sheet metal blocking the grimy windows, a counter, some parts shelves and racks, a couple of desks, and olive drab filing cases. Several large mean-faced men, necktieless in shabby suits, just standing around. Manny, a chubby, balding, older guy with stub of cigar, sat me down and leaned too close. A couple of the boys crowded around me, one of them — I swear it — nervously beating a length of lead pipe repeatedly into the palm of his hand. Was this life imitating art, or had I blundered into a Hollywood movie set? Hosea dissolved into the shadows.

Manny went into his spiel. Mrs. Winslow was a crazy. No way he could help her. They wrecked up everything. He'd really tried. He just wanted to make a living. The rent control made it impossible. Did I want him to close the place? Where would she live then? Where would any of them live? He couldn't afford this. He didn't need it. The rent was cheap, but even that she wouldn't pay. She took the money from welfare, why didn't she pay him? He'd close the building down, by God. He really would! Did I want to have to find them all new places to live?

"Listen," he told me, "all I want is for you to treat me the same as you treat her. I'm doing the best I can. Just treat me like you treat her." And as he said it he grasped my right hand in both of his, as though to entreat me for this simple fairness, and in his right hand was a crumpled wad of paper.

It gave me pause. Though I'd realized Hosea was on the take, I hadn't quite thought it through. Manny's left hand was encouraging my right to close, the big guy was banging that lead pipe into his meaty palm, they all leaned close and I thought fast. Me take a bribe? Me! They were kidding. But on the other hand, what the hell; if I didn't take it, the experience was just another boy scout outing in the city. Manny the slumlord, Dorathea the welfare creep, and me the phony West Coast liberal, playing at slum life in scuzz city.

I closed my hand.

Moments later I was out of there, after one more chorus of "All I want is for you to treat me the same as you treat her." Hosea reappeared and we made it back up Bushwick Ave. to the Mothers Day party, but it wasn't much fun any more. I took the train back to Manhattan, where I lived in a sixth-floor walkup on a Lower East Side street rattier even than Bushwick Ave. In my pocket, searching for change for the subway, I felt that wad of paper, like a knot in my soul. I wondered how much, but didn't unwad it. I listened inside my head for messages about how it felt to take a bribe. Another kind of virginity lost.

Two weeks later I finally opened the wad and found two $10s and a $5. Twenty-five bucks. I didn't even know whether to feel insulted or well paid. That's how dumb I was.

By the end of August I'd saved almost enough to get out of town. Then, in early September, Hosea Pendleton telephoned me at the welfare center. "Hey, man," he told me, "that Winslow woman is bugging Manny something fierce. He wants you to do like you promised."

Now was my moment of truth. I'd put off even thinking about it. "Oh yeh, right," I told him, talking on pure reflex. "That's just what I'm going to do. You tell him that I'm going to keep my promise. I said I'd treat him just like her, and I will. I'm not going to do a damn thing for either of them. I hope they drive each other nuts." Then I hung up. And none of the three of them ever called back.

I took the exact same two $10s and a $5, still crumpled together, and bought a typewriter — a handsome little 40-year-old Royal portable with chrome around the keys and a square black case — to take with me when I left. Which I did as swiftly as possible. Came home from my last day of work on a sunny payday afternoon in early October and by late the next day was halfway to Florida in a driveaway car.

I got as far as Jamaica, still another beautiful Caribbean island, where I lived in a handsome small town frozen in the year 1905, and learned a little of why people flee palm-tree poverty for the dream of a better life in Brooklyn. But I had to pay my karmic dues. The novel I drafted in Jamaica with that typewriter, and finished a year later back home in Oregon, the novel about life in the lower intestines of an almost imaginary enormous city, never was published. I loved it then, and I love it still, but my agent viewed it with disgust, and several editors with horror.

Does everybody get what they deserve? Would it have been different if I'd used another three pieces of paper to buy the typewriter? It seems unlikely. That's why I'm not ashamed that I took that bribe in Brooklyn. I've paid for it and I own it, its stillborn offspring is mine alone forever.

Invisible Ink

It's been used for millennia. Pliny the Elder, in the first century A.D., found it handy. Governments, spies, and diarists have all used it. Of course, children have long found invisible ink amusing and exciting.

Practice has shown the best ways to use the technology. George Washington, for instance, once berated an underling for sending a blank page with a message in invisible ink. According to George, the idea is to make the message appear innocent by using an innocuous letter with the invisible message between the lines. Another technique is to use the inside of an envelope for the secret message.

A fine nib is best. It's important to press lightly so that no indentation is left on the paper.

Low-tech solutions include milk or the juice of lemons or onions — all of which can be read by holding the paper near a lightbulb.

Some formulas use special chemicals. A luminous ink can be made by slowly heating a mixture of 30 grains of phosphorus with $1/2$ ounce of oil of cinnamon, which produces an ink visible in the dark. Ferric ammonium sulfate mixed with a small amount of water produces an ink that can be revealed by applying a dilute solution of sodium carbonate and water. A weak solution of copper sulfate makes an ink that turns light blue when exposed to ammonia fumes.

And here's a novel idea. Mix a pint of vinegar with an ounce of alum to make an ink that is used on the shell of a hard-boiled egg. Peel the egg to reveal the message (but don't eat the egg).

When we were preparing this book for press, we considered inserting several blank pages with secret writing on them. We didn't do that, but who knows, perhaps we put secret messages between the lines.

Interview With Keri Hulme

Dennis Held

New Zealand writer Keri Hulme is best known for her 1984 novel *The Bone People*, which was published by Spiral Collective Number Five. The book was a runaway success in New Zealand, and it won the Pegasus Prize and the New Zealand Book Award in 1984 and the United Kingdom's most prestigious literary award, the Booker McConnell Prize, in 1985. Here in the United States, the novel continues to do well; it is still in print, and has sold nearly 165,000 copies in paperback, according to Viking editor Paul Slovak.

It's an odd book. It offers "a taste passing strange," Hulme says in the preface, a darkly funny tale that spins together poetry, Maori legend, and multiple points of view into a story of love and terror, loss and redemption. Many critics raved about the book's ambitious treatment of important themes, in a language that is "complex and pungent," as *The New York Times Book Review* put it. But others complained about the book's many dreams and visions, or Hulme's use of Maori words. In an interview with *Contemporary Authors*, Hulme points out that the "most negative criticisms have come from England, where, I think, many people took it as a personal affront that a book from an erstwhile colony could sneak/grab/steal/purloin/be given as a political gesture — anything but win — their premier literary prize."

I interviewed Hulme in Missoula, Montana, where she spoke in a rare public appearance at the third "In The Thoreau Tradition" conference. (Hulme noted in the *CA* interview, "Living the quiet life isn't a gimmick or a publicity stunt as far as I'm concerned. It is a necessity. It is my *life*.")

We met at breakfast, and she began with three cups of industrial-strength coffee. Hulme said, "When I say I have two, three cups in the morning, I have a specially-made coffee cup my sisters got me for one Christmas that's about that big" — her hand hovered a foot above the table — "that holds nearly a pint. But don't show me as a caffeine addict, because I don't drink coffee thereafter. That's my charge to turn me into a human being." She laughs a lot, and punctuates her speech with a favorite curse: "bloody hell," which comes out "ber-luddy 'ell."

Dennis Held: It seems a bit silly of me to talk to you about secrets, since that's what secrets are, after all, the things we don't talk about. But I'm interested in the way characters' secrets are revealed to the reader in The Bone People. *One of the big criticisms of the book, at least here in the States, is that Joe isn't a fully developed character, that we don't know enough about him. But the secrets about Joe's past are revealed almost as he allows* himself *to remember. He's not about to just sit there and spill his guts. How do these people reveal themselves to you as you're working on the book? You said it took 18 years of working on and off to get it right.*

Keri Hulme: Joe is a particularly good example of that. I should hasten to add that I wasn't working on the book that whole time. Some years it didn't get touched — it was just there and disturbingly alive in a drawer, but I didn't have the time to get at it. But I was lucky one year, I got a grant that gave me three months working at it, and a lot of things were worked out during that time, including the character of Joe, because I had spent most of the time on Kerewin and Simon and the relationship between them. Joe was a sort of cardboard ogre in the background, you know, he was nasty to his son and that was sufficient, initially. And then I started getting very curious about him. Why *should* he be so nasty? And very, very gradually, it was a process of thinking about Simon's character and how he would react to somebody who was just a cardboard ogre. It couldn't be like that, the man had to have some personal charm, some affection, he had to be a source of strength as well as danger.

And Joe did reveal himself as a very charming human being, who for historical reasons was also unable to control his temper when faced with something that was frustrating or deliberately defiant, which is what his kid was being most of the time. And it was literally that slow process of thinking of how people act to each other and why they act that way to each other. Something does happen, though, for me and I'm sure for everybody who writes, that when you start thinking on a character deliberately — and I do something else, I draw my people, so I get a good idea of how they look — they start to reveal themselves in ways you did not expect. I didn't know Joe wanted to carve or could carve, for instance, until quite late in the piece, and the fact that he had spent a couple of years in bed with poliomyelitis was a very late construction, and it more or less came from the character himself. I mean, why did he have these funny spindly legs? That literally came as the result of a dream. Joe was standing wrapped in a towel with this beautifully muscled torso, and as I looked down, here's this sort of stick man, and I said, oh, *that's* different. But there is sometimes a kind of logic inherent in dreams, and if you follow up those weak clues they can be quite intriguing.

DH: Do the paintings help reveal the characters to you?

KH: Oh, yes, extraordinarily so. One of the unpleasant ones which hasn't to do with *The Bone People* happened with the new book. In *Bait*, everybody is hiding something, and some of the secrets are awesome and some of the secrets are puerile, but they all are hiding something. Hollis, this very large fish-and-chip cook who is extraordinarily mechanically deft and is a consummate fisherwoman, has a small son, a four-year-old, called the Nikli. He's not referred to as anything else, and whenever you ask why, the Nikli will simply say, that's my name; Hollis will say that's what he's called, and you don't get very

97

much further ahead. Anyway, I drew them, and he's one of the red-headed islanders — that's somewhat unusual. Every time I drew him there was a shadow that was *completely different*, and I realized the Nikli was something else as well as somebody else altogether. Hollis is not what she seems either, but that's one of my big surprises, I hope, and I don't want to give away any secrets, do I?

DH: I'd like to talk a little about secrets. I thought much of The Bone People *is about how we live with our own secrets...*

KH: Yes!

DH: And even how we keep secrets from ourselves, and how they have a way of making themselves known. Secrets can have both destructive and constructive powers, depending on how they're used. Do you know things about your characters that you don't feel you should reveal to the reader? Are there things you withhold?

KH: Just taking *The Bone People* again, that thing was very, very long at one stage. It was past 1700 pages. I went back — this was in the late seventies — and pursued the backgrounds for everybody. I made up family trees for them. I wrote stories, only one of which has been published, about them, that had nothing to do with what went on in *The Bone People*. And, yes, in the end they turned out to be irrelevant to the drive of the novel, so I suppose you could call those secrets withheld. I know my characters very intimately and thor-oughly. And the same with *Bait* — that's already happened, it has managed to spawn another novel from the material I kicked out of it.

The other thing is that you can think you have conveyed more of a character than the reader perceives. But because you've used — and everybody has them — your own private codes, your own loaded words, they haven't necessarily been picked up by other people.

DH: You've become a public figure and some things are known about you, some of your secrets have been...

KH: *Exposed*, yes. My fondness for large rings, for instance.

DH: Well, that's fairly self-evident. You've talked about how the Maori influences came down to you through your mother's family. Are there are things that you know about, spiritual matters, that don't make their way into your writing?

KH: Yes. There has been ever since — well, ever since forever, but particularly within the period of European contact there has been a very deliberate sequestering of some matters. There was incidentally a withholding of knowledge of some things from the general populace. There was something called the *Io cult, Io-matua-kore*, and this was an idea that really all the departmental gods, which the ordinary people knew about, sprang from something that really didn't exist, and was the private property of a certain class of priest and of the aristocracy. It was their particular cult.

As well as that each particular tribe has its own beliefs — you have places you don't show to outsiders, ideas you might touch on among yourselves but you don't begin to tell, because they are regarded as having their own particular inherent power, and if you let them out that power will drain away, and the support they give to your people will also drain away. In *The Bone People*, you might remember something called the *mauri*, and this is a common concept. I've seen one of our tribal *mauri* for a certain fish, and the spirit of the entire species of fish is supposed to reside in that, and if you damage it, you damage all those fish. There is no such thing as a *mauri*dom, the idea of the spirit for the entire country, but I figured okay, I can fix that. And that's what you can do also — with particular concepts that are withheld from the people at large — you can extrapolate from them.

We made a distinction — there are *purakau*, the stories you tell at winter, which include the Maori tales, doings of exceptional lovers, people who ran away to a tragedy, stuff like that. But there was another class of story altogether that wasn't really a story. It was always done in a chant, and very, very few of those are recorded indeed. Unfortunately, they have now devolved down to certain families, and those families are getting smaller, and the people who know them are getting older, so they will die with them. But that's the proper way for it to go, I think. I don't think they should be put down on a tape like that and then just let out.

Aside from anything else, we have a very strong belief that words can do damage. There is in fact a saying, that you can turn aside a spear of wood, but you can't turn aside a spear from a tongue. And once you let words loose, even in the printed medium, you can do damage to people who are entirely innocent. There was an extraordinary situation in the late 1980s when a feminist collective put together what was called *The Woman's Painting Book*, and it was all women artists from New Zealand. Several of us who were of Maori and also of Cook Island descent withdrew from it when in the book a *Pakeha* woman revealed that she used menstrual blood in her paintings. This is such a no-no-no that we figured it was possible, the fact that it was recorded, it could have damaged young people who wouldn't have known that — it might seem eccentric and very silly.

DH: Using the blood is prohibited, or talking about it?

KH: No, she had representation of her paintings that had used her menstrual blood. This curious idea of words having a potency that continues long after the page that they were written on has been burned seems to be intrinsic to other Polynesian cultures. I certainly know it's there in Samoa. They get very, very careful about that sort of thing. If you don't let those things out, they can't get appropriated by anybody. I think it's meant to be, intended to be, a compliment, but there have been a lot of *Pakeha* artists who have read Maori motifs and used them, and sometimes they do it in a way that is risible because they don't understand the meaning of them and put them in highly inappropriate places.

DH: You have one in mind.

KH: Ahh — yes I do. (Laughs.) Drawn signs are called *kowhaiwhai*, and there's a particular *kowhaiwhai* that represents the genitalia of a female ancestor. And you find these in meeting houses, and when you see that you know that that's intended to indicate that the pole below it is a female, and she's the ancestor of this particular group of people. And a *Pakeha* artist who certainly didn't know the meaning of that had drawn a rather startling portrait of a warrior with a flourishing *paihau* on his cheeks. (Belly-laughs.) Female genitals! And every Maori who saw it knew about it and started laughing. Somehow, unfortunately, word reached back to him and he withdrew that lithograph very quickly.

DH: I know you don't like to talk about books-in-progress, but Bait *is finished, isn't it? So we can talk about that?*

KH: We can talk about that. Envisage a settlement — you can't call it a village, it's too small for that — which has roughly twelve permanent residents and a hotel/tavern that caters to fishers, particularly people who are involved in trout fishing, and whitebaiters. And this settlement is basically fading away as the older, more permanent residents die off.

There are six pivotal characters. I don't want to give too much away, because it's a very interwoven novel, a tangle where people start to die off in alarming ways. It really is a book that deals with death, and with fishing, and with Tui [a main character]. It's the loss of her people, there's nobody else literally left of her particular tribe. She has nobody she can hand on her knowledge to. The person she's carefully cultivating kills himself in a kayaking accident. The easiest way I find to describe *Bait* is that if you can call *The Bone People* a love story, then *Bait* is a funny story about death and fishing. And that's funny ha-ha and funny peculiar.

DH: Tell me about the title.

KH: It's called *Bait* for several reasons, not least because the main action in the book takes place during a whitebaiting season — and that in New Zealand runs between August the 15th and the end of October. It is incidentally set slightly into the future.

DH: Well, that's contemporary then.

KH: Yeah. I just hope it doesn't get too contemporary. I postulate a little war with Indonesia and all sorts of things.

DH: I said we would talk about fishing and we haven't. Tell me a secret about whitebait fishing.

KH: Should I?

DH: Not a real secret, but a public kind of secret.

KH: Okay. One of the very simple and seemingly obvious secrets about whitebait netting — you use, incidentally, a roughly six-foot-long, foot-and-a-half-wide ovalish net frame that has a twelve-foot pole attached to it — one of the obvious secrets, but nobody who's a newcomer to the sport seems to pick it up, is that whitebait actually notice something that large glinting in the water, and if you put a piece of black PVC pipe 'round it they don't notice it quite so well and you catch remarkably more shoals of whitebait. Now, the next secret will cost ten dollars…. (Laughs.)

DH: I don't even know what they look like.

KH: They are what — five, six centimeters long — about three inches, very thin, and absolutely translucent except for a speckling along each side in a very fine line, where the lateral line is. And they have great silver eyes.

DH: Do you dry them, and…

KH: No! You just eat the entire fish — delicious cooked in a little butter with a bit of salt and pepper.

DH: Do you cast the net, or set it?

KH: There are several ways of doing it. You can have pop nets, you can have net frames that are lowered down into the big baiting waters further south. They have very elaborate wooden structures and cranes they use to lower their nets and bring them up again. I mean they can catch over a ton a tide so they need such things. Using our net we meet incoming surf, so you're holding the net against the incoming wave and hoping to sieve out as much bait as you can. There are other places where you have set nets with screens, a lot of places still where you have pop nets. There's a whole whitebait culture that I find obsessively interesting.

DH: And so you wrote a book about it.

KH: Part of the book is very definitely about whitebaiting. And I've written articles about it and I've written poems about it and I've written stories about it. In fact, I'll probably be remembered as the poet of the whitebait. Incidentally, the Japanese also write haiku about whitebait. There's a lovely one — who's it by? — it's not Basho — but it's "The whitebait, as though the spirit of the waters were moving." It really does look like that when you see them, they flicker kind of like translucent ghosts.

DH: Are you still living in your eight-sided house?

KH: I won't ever properly leave it, I don't think. I've actually got instructions in my will for my family to burn it down after I've cleared everything out, because it's so much a part of me. I did not only build it, but you put a lot of yourself into that kind of building. However I will be shifting for part of the year to the other side of the island, only because there's a lot of young members of my family growing up that I don't have very much contact with, and because we've now got heaps of tourists where I live and for about four months of the year that place is crowded.

DH: Is that a recent development?

KH: Yes it is. It really got going when they sealed the road into our place. Then you had all the camper vans and the bus traffic.

DH: I'm all in favor of gravel roads, for just that reason.

KH: I *love* them, I love them. I didn't realize how much I'd miss it. But you'd get people coming down the tar seal and they'd see the gravel and do a U-turn around the triangle and out again.

DH: It sounds like a project for you, desurfacing the road.

KH: We try, we try, you know — pickax a few potholes and see if they wash out, but they don't.

DH: Thank you. You've been very kind.

KH: Hey, feed me enough coffee, and I'm yours.

Why I Came to Write

David Xiao

1

Secrets, by definition, exist in present time — the things being hidden are being hidden now. However, most if not all secrets refer to events from the past, they are histories large and small kept under wraps, once-upon-a-time narratives sealed off, cut off, from the present.

A secret is like a knife which severs the flow of time, leaving a scar which will sometimes masquerade as the secret itself.

2

My father fled to Hong Kong in 1948, just before the People's Republic was established in China. He met my mother shortly after he arrived in the tiny British colony, and the two were married eleven years later in a church on Kowloon side. Although my father came from a big family — he had fifteen brothers and sisters in all — none of his relatives attended his wedding. He left them behind when he escaped the mainland.

Like most refugees — from anywhere and in anytime — my father rarely spoke of the past. When I was a boy my father never mentioned anything to me about his own boyhood; it was his secret, something which he felt belonged to him and him alone. So as I grew up in Hong Kong I did not know the name of the town where my father was born, or that he had fifteen siblings. I did not know his father's and mother's names, although this latter omission was actually quite normal, or at least traditional. As a rule, Chinese people are not supposed to mention their parents' names, especially not to their own children. I did not know my maternal grandfather's name until I read it on his tombstone, and when I first saw it I was too young to read the three characters carved onto the stone and my mother refused to read them for me. Keeping your parents' names a secret was a traditional filial expression, just as in the past commoners were never allowed to gaze directly at the emperor's face.

3

Most of my schoolmates in Hong Kong had pictures of elder kin hanging on the walls of their homes. Many of them had red and golden altars prominently displayed in their living rooms, small shrines dedicated to ancestors seen and unseen. Sweet smelling joss sticks burned inside those tiny household altars day and night. On special occasions my friends would stuff chunks of smoldering sandalwood into a ceremonial kiln and place it directly in front of the altar. The pungent odor filled their apartment for weeks.

But our family didn't have one of these ancestral shrines. My father was a Lutheran minister who thought filial worship a form of pagan superstition, and in any case we didn't have any ancestors that I knew of. To me, our family past was like that phantom hand crippled soldiers talk about — it was not there anymore, yet they could still feel it itching.

Perhaps my father's secrecy about his past was an expression of old fashioned Chinese reserve combined with the fact that Lutherans do not believe in open confession. Or maybe his past was something he did not have time to talk about. My father worked twelve to sixteen hour days, seven days a week. He not only served on the pulpit but also on a dozen administrative boards, both religious and secular. He taught theology classes and was the president of a seminary. He wrote books and magazine articles, edited journals, and even composed hymns. My father also traveled regularly to Malaysia, Indonesia, Singapore, Taiwan, the Philippines, and for a while, Vietnam, ministering to the scattered

Christian communities within the vast Chinese Diaspora.

My father served in a church founded by a handful of converts who, like him, fled China shortly before the Communist Revolution. They were Lutheran ministers in a place where Lutherans are a minority. My father and his colleagues thought of themselves as apostles adrift in a wilderness, people who had to be self-reliant in order to survive. Only God was at their side. They had a lot of work to do, and lived for the here and now where they could. But most of all they lived for the future, for life after death and the kingdom that is to come.

There were entire weeks, sometimes entire months, when I wouldn't see my father even while we were living under the same roof. I was asleep by the time he came home and he was still sleeping when I left for school early the next morning. There were nights when I thought I heard him pacing about inside my bedroom, checking on me as I slept, but perhaps I was just dreaming.

4

When I was fifteen, my parents sent me away to America. It was for the sake of my future, they said. Hong Kong would revert to Chinese rule in 1997, and my parents did not want me to be there when the time came. Everything in Hong Kong would change irrevocably the day the Communists arrived. Everyone in Hong Kong knew that — they talked about it all the time. The future hung over their heads like a sword. It was a future fraught with uncertainty yet utterly precise in its chronology. The future would arrive on July 1, 1997, at exactly one minute past midnight.

I could understand generally why my parents sent me away, but I yearned for a specific, personal reason why I had to leave Hong Kong while they stayed behind. Yet I did not ask them for an answer nor had I expected them, especially not my father, to give me one. He was who he was, I thought. As my father, he was expected to think for me. And as his son, it was beyond me to question him.

So I left Hong Kong. During my first few years in America I lived in a rural town in northern Minnesota with a family friend, another

Lutheran minister my father met when he was studying in the United States. After graduating from high school I moved to Minneapolis.

5

Does the responsibility of keeping a secret rest solely on who guards the secret? Or does it also require others who do not, or cannot, ask the right questions to bring what is hidden into light? Do secrets require a conspiracy between he who knows and he who does not?

A few years ago my father was in California gathering material for a book about the Lutheran communities in central China prior to the Revolution. He had traveled halfway around the world to search for archival material because there no longer were any records in China itself.

Several months into his work, however, my father suffered a massive heart attack and within twenty-four hours underwent quadruple bypass surgery at Kaiser Memorial Hospital in Oakland. The doctors cut open my father's chest, took out his heart, and stopped it for forty-seven minutes. Within days of my father's traumatic but lifesaving operation, I flew to Oakland to be at his side. It was the first time I had seen him in years. His face was gaunt, his eyes sunken. He looked like those death masks in college anthropology books. Plastic tubes and electrical wires ran into and out of him.

Over the next several days I sat by my father's side and asked him to tell me something about his life. We looked at each other but did not touch. He spoke in hoarse whispers. I leaned down to hear what he said.

6

In the summer of 1969, a platoon of Red Guards gathered outside my fourth aunt's home in Sichuan Province. In preceding years, Mao's Young Generals arrested and "disappeared" several of her older brothers and sisters and the Generals were now coming for her. The crimes my uncles and aunts had been accused of pertained to their family history: their father, my grandfather, had been a Lutheran minister back in the 1930s and '40s. The Party had officially branded him as an opium peddler, one who sold drugs to the spirit. Even though my grandfather died eight years before the People's Republic was established, and had been dead for twenty-six years by the time the Cultural Revolution rolled around, the Red Guards remembered him. They said he betrayed his race and his culture.

My fourth aunt was Party cadre in the city of Chengdu. Although she was a labor organizer and longtime member of the Communist party, her official status wasn't enough to protect her from the Red Guards. Those teenagers had no respect for such things. To them, my aunt's error was not in her resume or even in her mind. Instead, it was in her blood. So they dragged my aunt out into the street and began kicking and beating and whipping her like an animal, torturing her in front of her husband and their three young daughters.

Until my father began telling me this terrible story, I did not know I had a fourth aunt, or any aunt for that matter. And in 1969 we were living in New York City, in Greenwich Village (we lived there for five years while my father was studying for his Ph.D. at N.Y.U.). I was five years old at the time, and my memories of that summer include watching Neil Armstrong walk on the moon and seeing Mao Zedong — who was trying to put a new man on the Earth — swim across the Yellow River for the second time in a decade. Both Mao and Armstrong had performed their feat on TV. I also remember seeing photographs of Red Guards in *Life* magazine; they were thrusting their fists and little red books up in the air, all the while sobbing for the camera. I did not know what those people were doing, however. To me, they were just pictures in a magazine.

My father did not know what was going on in China either. Although he used to receive letters from home on a semi-regular basis, occasionally ending up with someone else's mail because government censors stuffed the wrong letter back into the envelope, after the Cultural Revolution started, all correspondence from China ceased. My father was left in the dark. So during the summer of 1969, he decided to write to his fourth sister in Chengdu and ask her what was going on. Because she and her husband were both Party cadres, my father figured she had enough clout to pierce the shroud of secrecy.

A postman in Chengdu delivered my father's letter to my aunt's house just as the Red Guards were torturing her on the street. The timing was like that of a scene in some melodramatic movie. The leader of the Red Guard platoon, as soon as he saw the letter was postmarked from the United States of America, snatched it from the postman and began waving it to the crowd that had gathered outside my aunt's home, saying this was material proof of her connection to imperialist running dogs. The Guard then tore the envelope open and began reading the letter out loud, sneering all the while.

The content of the letter wasn't what the Guard had expected, however. Instead, it was almost entirely composed of mundane niceties about the weather in New York City and innocuous information about our family life in Greenwich Village. Not once did my father mention the Cultural Revolution or American astronauts walking on the moon, nor did he ask my aunt any questions. And his last sentence read, "Fourth Sister, if you find yourself in difficult times, be inspired by the courage of Mao Zedong. Think of him swimming heroically across the Yellow River."

The language which the Young General had so mockingly read to the crowd had turned out to be his own. Embarrassed, perhaps even frightened, the teenager quickly stuffed the letter back into its envelope and dropped it on the ground, right next to my bleeding aunt. Then he and the other Guards left.

7

This, I have come to believe, is the essential purpose of writing. It is something which keeps people alive.

8

My fourth aunt told my father that story in 1979, the year he revisited China for the first time in over three decades. In 1979, Deng Xiaopeng came to power and a new constitution was ratified by the Central Politburo, guaranteeing, among other things, religious freedom to citizens of the People's Republic. Deng's government had invited my father to Beijing because it wanted religious, social, and political leaders from around the world, but particularly from Hong Kong, to witness the changes it said it was rendering. The Chinese government wanted to show people from Hong Kong that its reforms were real; the future was in better hands now; they need not worry about 1997 anymore.

My father informed the United Front, the Party's propaganda bureau, that he would agree to go to Beijing if it would let him visit his mother in Hunan Province. At the time, people in Hong Kong were still not allowed to enter the interior provinces of China. The bureau agreed and so my father went, first to Beijing, and then home.

As he wandered through the streets of Beijing, my father came across a boyhood friend whom he had not seen in almost thirty years. He and my father were from the same hometown, Yiyang, and both had attended a nearby seminary together when they were teenagers. My father and this man, along with two other friends from Yiyang, were among the forty or so young seminarians who evacuated to Hong Kong at the end of 1948, just before the People's Liberation Army gained control of the central Yangzi valley. My father told me that he and his three friends had made a pact to return to China as soon as they graduated. Unlike the American and Scandinavian missionaries who moved the seminary out of China before Marshal Zhu De's armies arrived, the four of them were sympathetic to and inspired by the Revolution back home. The Party's language of national salvation mirrored their own, and like so many young Chinese during those years, they had high hopes for the newly established People's Republic.

My father and his three friends had their future all planned out, but history doesn't take personal reservations. His friends completed their religious studies a year before he did and returned home without him. They couldn't wait anymore, my father said. The Bamboo Curtain went up shortly after his friends crossed the border, and over the next thirty years neither he nor anyone else in Hong Kong heard from those three men again. It was as if they had vanished from the face of the Earth.

My father and his old friend stood on opposite sides of the street. They stared at each other for a long time. Neither of them said a word. But as my father began crossing to the other side, his friend held up his palm and mouthed the word "stop" before he turned and ran away.

The following day a taxi driver drove by the hotel where my father was staying and secretly handed him a letter. It was from his friend. The letter recounted how he and his two classmates had been arrested as soon as they reached Hunan Province. The local authorities charged them with espionage and asked them to confess, but they refused and were then taken to separate cells and tortured. This went on for months, the man wrote, until his interrogator finally told him that his two friends had not only confessed to their own crimes but had implicated him as well. As a reward for their honesty and cooperation they had been set free. It was now his turn to confess, the interrogator said, so that he, too, could be released. And in any case they already knew everything so there was nothing left for him to hide.

The man did as he was told, and he was indeed let go later that day. But once he got out of prison he learned that his friends had not been released. Instead, the statement he signed was used against his friends, and a few days later the two were shot in the back of the neck during a public execution.

My father whispered it all into my ear.

In the days ahead he also told me that he served as a medic during the Sino-Japanese War, dressing wounds and changing bandages for Chinese soldiers retreating from the front. My father had no idea what he was doing — he was only eleven years old at the time — yet the Guomindang conscripts always addressed him as "doctor."

Besides caring for the wounded as best he could, my father also buried the dead. One summer, he and three other child medics were sent to a neighboring village after Japanese soldiers had massacred everyone there. The villagers' bodies laid on the ground for days. Most of them turned gray, others brown, some exploded in the heat. There were over three thousand corpses scattered across the village, and it took my father and his friends three days and three nights to burn them all. The four boys worked around the clock until their work was done.

9

A few months before my father's heart attack, I wrote to him informing him I wanted to be a writer. For years my father wanted me to become a doctor, but using language I knew he would understand, I told him being a writer was my calling.

As a college student I spent too much time writing about people who had no past, no ethnicity, and were living in indeterminate places and times. In a small hospital room in Oakland, my father gave me what I needed most in order to become a writer: facts. He gave me his own stories so they could become mine, so that one day I might make them my own. He was offering me material to make my dream come true.

My father was ready to let go of his secrets. I had asked to hear them and was ready to listen. A secret is at its most powerful when it is passed on. Its force is strongest at the moment of its release, and when absorbed it can power a person for life.

Your Life on a Chip, for Sale to the Highest Bidder

Charles Ostman

An Imminent Scenario

Consider this possibility: within the next few years, every aspect of your life — past and present — will be on a nationwide data base and encrypted onto a national ID card. You will be required by law to carry this ID card at all times and to show it on demand to the authorities. Unlike a driver's license, this will be the functional equivalent of an "existence license."

Computer systems, able to train themselves using the latest in artificial intelligence, will automatically scan the centralized data base for "undesirable or improper" lifestyle characteristics, and target those individuals for automatic monitoring.

Virtually all communication media will soon be 100 percent readable by computer, allowing automated monitoring based on pre-selected criteria without the need for specific human intervention, or court authorized permission. Physical surveillance of individuals will be possible, via satellite, from control centers thousands of miles away from the target. Individuals — even entire communities — will be observed, day and night, robotically. Pervasive surveillance of the general public at all public and private institutions will be considered the norm, and in many situations, possibly required by law.

Cyber stealth will become the new commodity for those who wish to be "off the grid." In a world where all encryption of data and communication will be regulated and authorized by the National Security Administration (NSA), and use or possession of non-authorized encryption for private use will become a federal offense, the ability to mask encrypted communication via the phone or the internet will be highly prized. Similarly, as digital cash replaces physical currency as legal tender for all transactions, an underground barter system will emerge.

This scenario doesn't begin to describe the list of major players. An enormous number of parallel interests are poised to use the newly available technologies. Previously dedicated to military/national security applications, there is a huge industrial base that must find new markets — public and private.

A staggering economic potential resides in this industry. Not since the Vietnam War has so much industrial and financial potential resided in a specific circumstance. Since ours has always been a war-based economy, and if the war on drugs has in fact hit the incarceration industry saturation point, the next growth industry will be a "war on personal freedom." Of course, it won't be called that.

Most of the public is neither remotely familiar with the technical details of such a system, nor are they likely to recognize its implementation even as it is occurring. But we need to know. It is like a very large, complex engine, with the key in the ignition, poised to be turned on. It emerges from a combination of factors and developments, any one of which alone would not be significant. However, the combination now, in a political climate favorable for "turning the key," makes this scenario not only possible, but inevitable.

Personal privacy has been considered sacrosanct, a constitutional right. Not that it ever really existed. But until recently, the technologies available to those agencies determined to violate the basic right to privacy were at least limited. Today, a drastic, encompassing change is at hand.

What propels this change? A combination of things: extremely sophisticated surveillance technology; pervasive digital information collection and exchange; a military-industrial complex eager to find new markets for its technologies; an enormous, multibillion dollar market potential for information database marketing services; and a government obsessed with ever tighter control over the activities of its citizens.

From deep personal involvement [See Ostman's biographical notes. Ed.] with cutting-edge artificial intelligence systems, optical computing, "smart" object recognition, machine vision, and other related technologies, I bring an insider's view of how far this has progressed, as well as an understanding of the socioeconomic and political factors involved in its current implementation.

I want to make clear that I am not suggesting a massive conspiracy, but rather portraying a logical series of progressions, the interactive results of a collection of industrial and governmental interests, a series of perceived security issues, and an enormous financial incentive for many participants. The implications are enormous.

For those who find the above scenario offensive or undesirable, there is an currently opportunity, if not for prevention, then at least for preparation for the inevitable. We are viewing the tip of a large iceberg. And before you dismiss this as the ravings of a paranoid lunatic bent on fantastic conspiracy theories (believe me, I wish it were) consider the following synopsis of current and near future technologies in their political context. Then, decide for yourself.

#

The recent attempt to issue a "public health card" (part of the Clinton health plan) could be construed as preparation for a general ID card that would eventually contain all aspects of one's life history. The step would be reasonable, since the elderly already have Medicare cards and we all have Social Security cards. To further test public acceptance of the general idea, this suggestion was rapidly followed by another, the "worker verification card," which was shown on national TV by Donna Shellela, Secretary of Labor. Perhaps the growing xenophobia over illegal immigrants will serve as a justification for the worker ID card.

Consider this carefully for just a moment. With these two trial balloons already floated before the public, how long will it be before the idea of combining both functions in the same card is proposed? Once this happens, it is merely a formality before access to anything, including currency, will be embedded in the same card.

What could be encoded? Information of interest and of substantial commercial and strategic value would include financial and tax records, genetic information (even an individual's entire DNA code), medical history (with particular emphasis on specific diseases, genetic predispositions, mental disorders, or substance abuse histories), political affiliations, subscriptions to certain publications, membership in various special interest groups, and sexual preferences or habits, just to mention a few.

This information has enormous commercial potential, as it will be marketed to information service agencies that will then sell specific database screening services to employers, law enforcement agencies, industrial and political groups, etc. In the wake of dramatic cutbacks in various military development programs, this new market for private and commercial security and surveillance technologies is seen as a viable transition industry. But the implications go far beyond commerce.

Many members of the Senate and Congress, as well as the President, are under extreme pressure from their constituencies to protect jobs and local economies from the consequences of military cutbacks. They see this type of industrial transition as crucial to saving their own political careers.

The concept of a centralized data-collection/personal-control mechanism is not new. But only now does the technical capability combine with specific perceived strategic needs to actually facilitate implementation.

Agencies of the federal government — the IRS, the Treasury Department, the NSA, the Drug Enforcement Administration, the FBI, various military intelligence agencies, etc. — are vying for access to such data. Furthermore, the traditional modalities of wire tapping, photo-surveillance, and the like that required human interaction and court issued warrants are giving way to automated, invisible surveillance and data scanning, which no longer fall under the current definitions of invasion of personal privacy. It is in this climate of political expediency that the "Big Brother" world so vividly detailed as fiction may become fact. All the requisite elements are there: a weak presidency desperate to court favor with the conservative elements of government; an enormous financial incentive for former military contractors to ply their trade; a plethora of government agencies that have been trying for years to implement these technologies and now see their big chance to bring these concepts to life; and most important, a public indoctrinated by an anticrime propaganda blitz, willing to blindly receive this new realm as acceptable — as the norm.

The Process of Implementation — A Chain of Events

Surveillance and monitoring will become ubiquitous over time. The following suggests how this may unfold:

1. The leading edge will be access to employment. A national ID/employment verification card will be required. Like the draft card of the recent past for men of military age, all citizens will have to carry it at all times when in public.

2. Other information service oriented agencies (Bureau of Census, IRS, etc.) will obtain the legal right to piggyback specific data sets onto the same card. Private organizations will begin to market data screening and analysis services to employers, insurance companies, etc.

3. At the same time that access to lawful employment will require this card, a parallel effort will integrate digital cash credits into the same card, replacing physical currency as legal tender, and creating a national, debit/credit currency system. Private banking systems will convert their existing ATM card services to be compatible with the new card.

4. Artificial intelligence software systems will automatically scan for and monitor unusual spending habits — or other indicators of

lifestyle activities that are outside of the statistical norm, based on the socioeconomic demographic profile of the monitored individual.

5. Federal law will require all private and public institutions to adopt the federal "identity, currency, and employment authorization card." The rationale will be economic emergency, crime and drug control, and illegal immigration control.

6. Taxation will occur as automatic deductions from the electronic currency account of each individual. Anyone who contests the IRS's taxation assessments will automatically be elevated to a special surveillance/monitoring status.

7. In the interests of national security, special surveillance status will quickly be extended to those who file lawsuits against the government, petition for information via the Freedom of Information Act, engage in protest activities, etc.

The Technologies

Current technologies already make most of the above possible. However, the accelerated pace of technological development will extend and enhance the possibilities. These are components of the potentially ubiquitous surveillance and monitoring system:

1. Both magnetic and holographic encoded optical storage media will be used in the national ID cards. The storage capacity of such media is more than sufficient to contain a complete dossier on one's entire life. To ensure that all information is current and unaltered, card data will be subject to required, government-authorized renewal on a periodic basis. In addition, information on the card will be encrypted.

A new class of low cost plastics, referred to as photo-reactive polymers, in development at the IBM Almaden Research Center, can provide holographic information storage equivalent to an entire encyclopedia in the area of an average postage stamp.

2. The Clipper chip (or a similar type of device that will ensure that a system is not altered in some unauthorized way) will be embedded in all personal computers, and be required under penalty of federal law to remain untampered with. Modification-detection

technology will actually reside within the chip and will trigger an on-line response should any tampering be attempted. Development of this technology is well advanced, particularly at Scandia National Laboratory (part of the national lab system that dates back to the days of the atomic bomb development programs, which is now under pressure to provide its federally financed R&D programs to the private sector).

3. All commercial computer encryption tools will be federally registered and authorized. Possession of unauthorized encryption/decryption capability will be punishable as a federal felony. This will apply to all internet data, digital phone calls, and all other bands of FCC regulated transmission.

4. Intelligent-video and multispectral surveillance equipment will be standard in virtually all corporate and government facilities, and may even be required in many instances. Artificial-intelligence-based, object-recognition systems will automatically scan for such criteria as facial characteristics and movement or activity cues. Both satellite and ground-based surveillance cameras, combined with this software, can automatically recognize and categorize targets without human intervention.

Based on biological modeling of the human eye, these so-called "smart staring infrared focal plane array" sensors (FPA's) are being developed by various research teams to "see" in both daylight and darkness. The Raytheon Corporation has developed "smart eyes" (under an Air Force contract) that can see, learn, and offer visual decision rendering based on real-time surveillance stimulus.

Miniaturization and low cost have made available credit card-sized devices that include not only a complete video camera system mounted on a circuit board, but more importantly, an on-board computer for instant image enhancement, feature detection, and related functions. An optional library of pre-stored feature data allows the camera to independently recognize such things as a specific face.

Automated Fingerprint Identification Systems (AFIS), voice analysis and recognition, and retinal scan information — all under the heading of biometric data processing — are being pursued by various vendors. This rapidly developing technology is making it affordable for most businesses to use extremely advanced surveillance and security systems. But of greater importance is the emergence of service bureaus that will provide on-line database access to one's personal dossier for any employer or other private interest. Already cited as potential clients by vendors of these services are prisons, banks, military bases, research facilities, pharmaceutical houses, and corporations.

Furthermore, intelligent live-scan systems are foreseen for department stores, supermarket checkout lines, ATM sites, and so on. The FBI already utilizes a live-scan fingerprint verification system at its National Criminal Information Center (NCIC) and has a library of over 250,000 fingerprints on file. It has stated an interest in expanding its capabilities by tying its current database to the national healthcare card system. If this policy were implemented, it would drastically increase the size of the NCIC database, essentially making all healthcare recipients part of the NCIC processing system.

5. Global surveillance of individuals is on the agenda. The geosynchronous satellite network, proposed as a global communication system, will simultaneously serve as a platform for surveillance of any coordinate on Earth's surface. Ultra high resolution visual and infrared technologies currently allow observation of any area to a resolution of two-inch square from orbit, day or night.

The Clinton administration reversed a long-standing government policy by allowing commercial access to what was once considered classified, so-called spy satellite data transmissions. This was the result of extreme pressure from industrial groups who are poised to market surveillance data services.

Congressman George Brown of California, head of the House Science and Technology Committee, has facilitated a commercial market for high-resolution satellite-image data. Not surprisingly, many of the major technology contractors of both satellite and surveillance equipment (General Dynamics, Raytheon, McDonnell Douglass, Lockheed, etc.) and large scale database processing services (TRW, Equifax, Bank of America, etc.) with huge financial stakes in this situation are California-based corporations.

The Department of Commerce specifically cites a $5–8 billion industry arising from the marketing of satellite surveillance related products and services. Competition from countries such as Germany, Israel, France, China, and even Russia — all vying for the low cost commercial satellite launch and surveillance services market share — have stimulated an extreme sense of urgency among many in the United States to capture as much market share as possible. General Merrill A. McPeak, US Air Force Chief of Staff, stated that by the year 2000, over 30 countries will have remote sensing satellites in orbit and be marketing their services.

The Technology Reinvestment Program (a Congressionally sanctioned and financed mandate) has currently reviewed over 2800 development proposals, representing $8.5 billion — programs specifically targeted at commercial markets for technologies that were previously of military origin. At the top of the list were commercial applications for security, surveillance, law enforcement, and strategic data analysis and processing.

Teledisc, founded by Bill Gates and Craig McCaw, envisions a system of 840 geosynchronous-orbit satellites, in which virtually all aspects of global communication digital media will be accessible by anyone, anywhere, for a fee. To justify this $9 billion project, a large array of potential clients are being aggressively courted in advance. Should this scheme be fully developed, there would be no single area on the face of the planet that could not be seen. And more importantly, virtually all digital communications would be linked through this universal transponder system. This would provide access to virtually all electronic communications. Both Bill Gates and Craig McCaw refused to be interviewed by *Scientific American* on this topic.

6. Closer to the Earth's surface, expect surveillance by unmanned, robotic devices, both airborne and land-based, with the ability to observe an individual or a dwelling from a distance, day or night. They can also monitor certain communications via RF (radio frequency) signature in a broad spectrum of wavelengths. These vehicular devices, particularly airborne, can be called up from a distant control center (thousands of miles away from the target), sent

to the target zone, and the surveillance data can be collected and examined in near real time via satellite link.

Presently, robots are beginning to replace human security personnel. A new device can patrol a region of up to 15 square miles for 12 hour shifts (between charges), utilizing an ultrasonic sensing system to navigate around complex obstacles, and featuring onboard both optical and infrared visual situation evaluation capabilities. An operator at a remote site can control and interact with a group of these.

The High Altitude Long Endurance unmanned aircraft development program, part of NASA's collection of general robotic and unmanned craft projects, is focused on producing a series of flying platforms that can stay airborne for days at a time, and can carry a payload of advanced optical and infrared camera systems. These remotely controlled devices can be deployed by an operational command center thousands of miles from the actual surveillance target.

The Department of the Navy is currently soliciting research on a "fuzzy logic" based communications signal/signature analysis system that can recognize the content of any transmitted signal from anywhere, regardless of electronic countermeasures. Among specific commercial applications cited in the solicitation are "law enforcement, surveillance, drug interdiction." The Navy is also actively soliciting a robotic, flyable platform for optical and infrared surveillance. The potential commercial applications cited are "riot control, border surveillance, personnel detection."

7. The technical limitations that were once enormous barriers to nationwide personal data processing and storage no longer exist. Much of it is readily available and reasonably inexpensive. The next stage is being set. For instance, the Department of Commerce is financing a joint project to develop the type of system required for nationwide population monitoring. To handle the instant processing of such awesome amounts of data, more powerful computers are required. Research sponsored by NASA at the Jet Propulsion Laboratory is producing the Hyperswitch Communication Network computer — the *ultimate* supercomputer.

Back at street level, vendors are already offering affordable components that give personal computers a thousand times improved performance in pattern recognition processes. A networked array of such machines puts extremely robust cognitive process engines into the hands of even mid-sized commercial clients, bringing cutting-edge benefits to the largest commercial base.

Smarter computers. Self-training computers. The surveillance potential of this new generation of machines and software is virtually unlimited.

Extensive research at NASA's Jet Propulsion Laboratory is intended to create a self-training data classification system that not only analyzes tasks and recognizes events, but has the ability to assess the relative importance of information observed by the system.

Already on the market is a "DataBase Mining Workstation," which looks for interesting data sets on its own, according to features of interest defined by the client. The system, once trained, automatically tracks anything (or anyone) that gets its attention. An "intelligent" credit card fraud and abuse detection system can already automatically search for and learn about unusual spending habits and related behavior. Clients for this system currently include AT&T, Colonial National Bank, Eurocard Netherland, First USA Bank, Household Credit Services, and Wells Fargo Bank. Automated credit risk evaluation, the equivalent of "credit redlining" is perceived as the next level of client services from this technology.

8. Automated voice recognition can be activated upon a predetermined cue to digitize, store, and convert into text any monitored speech. For instance, a person engaged in a phone conversation, who may already be on a list because of previous political, drug-related, or other activities, could be monitored by this automated recognition system, which would begin to digitize and store text files if a certain phrase or collection of keywords were spoken.

The Department of the Navy, under its "Global Surveillance and Communications" technology solicitations, has requested research to develop the capability for "robust signal processing of speech," and specifically cites "voice communications countermeasures and counter-counter measures" as part of a comprehensive, speech recognition/processing system.

Under commercial development is a telephone call-processing and automated speech recognition system, including "automatic keyword and phrase" recognition. This is useful for workforce screening and monitoring, and "workflow automation" processes, as is a technique for analyzing and storing the transmission "signature" of *every telephone* on a nationwide communication system. The initial application is fraud prevention in telephone systems, but this technology is easily adapted to other applications using identity markers and feature recognition.

Conclusion

Though this might seem like clichéd stuff of a rehashed *1984* scenario, the difference is that for the first time in history, the technology is available to design and implement an encompassing surveillance system. The political will is most certainly at hand, and it is being cleverly disguised in the wrappings of politically acceptable solutions to perceived public problems. With the bombing of the federal building in Oklahoma City, the furor over militia groups— and indeed anyone who might want to question authority — is ushering in a new wave of Congressional mandates to accelerate the trend toward revised interpretations of constitutional rights of privacy. Such emotional appeal is an apparently timeless technique. After all, the threat of child pornography on the internet recently made the idea of monitoring all internet content an acceptable idea.

This is not simply a "government spying on me" conspiracy issue, though it is that, too. The issue is control. In other words, when you apply for a job, the company in question will know everything about you — even genetic information, sexual orientation, medical and psychological event data, previous financial information, etc. — because it will be embedded into your information/ID/employment/currency card. There is an entire industrial community of information providers who will make billions of dollars from the marketing of your data. They want the scenario I've described made legal and made theirs as soon as possible.

Even without the law enforcement agencies of our government, the private sector has strong allies in the public sector. The Federal Reserve Board has been waiting for a chance to implement a cashless currency system for years. The IRS, for obvious reasons, is equally anxious to see this process come to life.

Is there a remedy short of a fundamental change in who decides and how? Probably not, but that doesn't mean we have to cooperate or take it lying down. Much of the underlying technology is in place and active already. We can slow the complete implementation and begin devising ways to regain some of our privacy. For instance, methods of encryption that can pass government monitoring undetected is one example. But of a much greater importance will be the rapid evolution of an underground, cashless, barter system society. There will be no other reasonable way for people to avoid the large-scale use of digital cash — and the surveillance built into it. Once electronic cash becomes the accepted norm, we can expect that all physical currency will be required to be turned in to authorized banking facilities in exchange for electronic cash credit units accessible via your newly issued national ID/information/currency unit access card. The government decides what constitutes legal tender, so there remain areas where there will be political resistance. And the question arises, however, to what extent can various legal sanctions against casual barter actually be enforced. The current massive underground economy suggests otherwise.

Just remember: It's not only the secrets kept from us that matter, but our ability to have secrets of our own.

Photography
of the Invisible

Cherie Hiser

The seeds for my thirty year inquiry into other peoples' worlds were planted when I was a young girl during conversations with my father at the dinner table on our farm in rural Oregon. Part of me was an innocent, sheltered, only child while the other part was quite worldly at 10 and 11-years old. I experienced World War II, beginning to end. I grew up on naval bases. From 5 to 8-years old. I lived at the Sacred Heart Convent, where my parents thought they could protect me from the racial diversity of a public school. I survived the San Francisco earthquake; I once saw a dead woman pulled from the surf; I watched a cougar kill my dog; and a childhood friend and I spent almost a year walking home from school with rocks in our shoes, preparing for the pain of childbirth. But I didn't know, nor had I seen people unlike myself.

Dad was prejudiced about most people who were different in any way, and our 1950s dinnertime conversations were about teaching me his values. Mom didn't say a word. I knew later it was because she didn't agree. I argued. I cried. I fought. I couldn't accept his narrow-mindedness even though I had never met a black or a yellow person, nor had I seen a tattooed person, a biker, a homeless person, a foreigner. This philosophical battle continued for 40 years. And he held tight to his beliefs.

I went on to spend thirty years with a camera in my hands, trying to change his mind although he rarely looked at my photographs. I wanted to convince him we are all the same. Not only did I photograph others, I lived as one of them, spoke their language, shared their experience. I immersed myself as far into their demimondes as I could in an obsessional documentation. In my own life I loved a Japanese man, a Native American man, a transsexual man. I married a man with a full body tattoo. I lived in a gay community. And I've worked in psychiatric hospitals for 17 years.

I take two pictures of each subject. The first is how I thought my dad would want to see the person: attractive, confident, "normal." The second photograph is the subject's secret. In my fantasy my dad — and society — will be drawn to the individual by how they look. I want the stigma to disappear, to make the unordinary ordinary.

At eighty years old, my father changed to become a loving humanist. He said he was tired of fighting. His fight created my life's work: "The Odyssey of the Invisible." He is gone now...but we still have lively conversations over Friday meatloaf, canned asparagus, dehydrated mashed potatoes, and sliced brown bananas floating in red Jello.

Peggy I, 1983

Peggy II, 1983

Mae I

Mae II

Masa in Vienna I, 1979

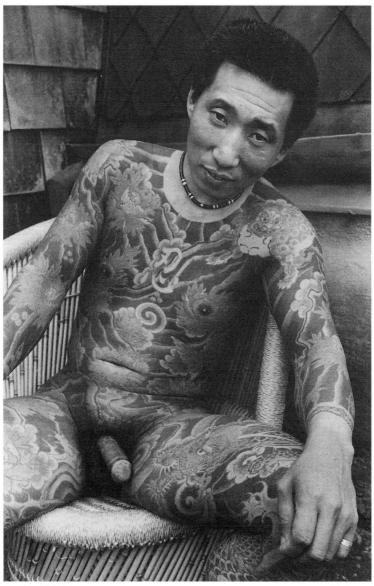

Masa in Vienna II, 1979

Elizabeth I, 82 years old

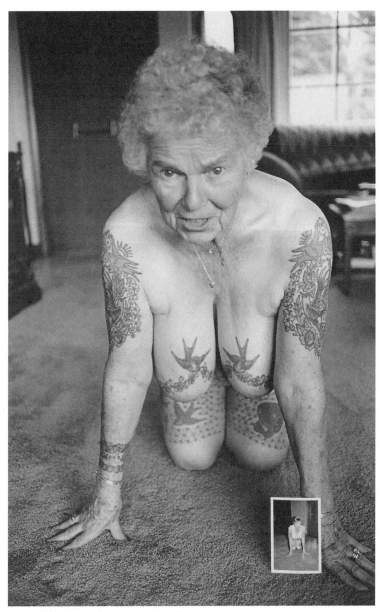

Elizabeth II, with inset picture from 1950

Characteristics of Secret Societies

Our research suggests, not surprisingly, that secret societies differ for men and women, reflecting power and control in the general culture. For women, rituals of initiation and membership often serve to separate them, emphasizing their individuality or their responsibility to the general society dominated by men and providing little in the way of either solidarity or group organization. Women's societies frequently serve as auxiliaries to the men's. For men, the opposite is usually the case, with the rituals emphasizing group solidarity and preparing them for life and leadership in the political arena.

Virtually all secret societies maintain strict hierarchies, with higher levels of participation determined by such distinctions as age or achievement of prescribed goals. Revelation of "deeper" secrets accompanies advancement in most hierarchies.

The secret knowledge shared by members of a society has an almost public face in the signs and signals used by initiates to identify one another. These may be handshakes, gestures, or key words.

In all secret societies there are penalties defined for revelation of any of the secrets. These range from merely embarrassing to fatal.

Snake River Drawdown

Nance Van Winckel

A boy I loved had gone and asked my father
for a letter. He was after a military career.
  They'd just begun to draw the river down.
  Down past Clarkston and Red Wolf.
    Sockeye left to flail and float
    in a bed of cracked mud.

My father's face wore a calm on the surface.
He'd stood by the river when it was a river.
  Close to our window, he'd paced long past
  midnight. A daughter, in black armband,
    was out late with a boy who claimed
    he was after his country's good.

But he'd struggled with me in the river.
Until I quit. I was tired. No longer sure what
  the fighting was for. Something black slid
  from my arm, disappeared down the rapids.
    Afterwards we sat by a water stretched low
    and sinking, no longer wild, or roaring.

Now he'd come home to its carcasses and putrid
sludge. A last pair of bald eagles picked at bad fish

tangled in tree stumps. My father's ghost paced
one bank of the river. And stripped of his stripes,
     the lieutenant paced the other. Then he stopped;
     he helped men pull a body from the shallows.

I stood with the women and watched.
Once, from out there, he'd come for me,
     rising, hand over slow hand, and dripping.
     It was a river of our own devising. The body,
          when they lifted it, was shreds. No one knew
          who it was, and no one was missing.

The World Made Whole and Full of Flesh

Sallie Tisdale

Summer is coming on as I watch — bearing crickets, dust, carnal iris flags. The baby maple we'd given up for dead shows sudden leaves, limp on thin branches. Spring grass shimmers in the light and from my seat on the shaded porch I can see the big spiders in its unkempt length run from shadow to sun, sun to shadow. A car raises the dirt on the road a few hundred yards distant. People always take that corner too fast, and get a scare; they have to slow all at once and pull hard on the wheel. Sometimes I can see a pale face go by, concentrating, listening to the brakes tighten and hold with a long, thin cry.

I reach for my papers, shifting in the wooden chair, and hear its hammer feet scrape sharply across the porch. I do very little on these still, hot days; I read, but not well, whatever is at hand, and the neatly printed words rise up like vapor and are gone, into air so hot and blue it seems a windowpane of solid light.

The telephone rings and I get up and go in the dim house to answer. The musty, unused room smells of acrid wood smoke and field dust; the faded carpet around the stove is littered with pale yellow chips. I tell the caller that Paul is in the fields. I can see him there, small and far away, through the old warped window glass. He is getting ready to plant the summer wheat, bending and lifting, streaked with dirt. After I hang up, I look around the room and think I'll clean the house, pick some flowers for the table, but I don't. I find it hard to work here, to change a single thing in this big strange house, to make sounds into words, words into all that isn't spoken. Even in the evening, when David or Alan or Lee come to call or we leave for town — even when we talk for hours, words seem less important than the spaces between them. Words take apart time, and time is all I have here. The silence here is pendant and strong, draped over the days, and suddenly it's more than I can bear. I reach for the radio and listen through the static to the meaningless news.

There are only the two of us in this big old house, and sometimes only Paul. I only visit — and many people visit Paul. When I come, the house is always the same, as though no one was ever here, as though no one but Paul had lived here in the hundred years the fine old farmhouse has been standing. Paul pays scant attention to its details — to its big beams and tongue-and-groove siding and sunny rooms. He attends to the dirt instead. Most of the rooms haven't been used in years, and when I'm here I spend my afternoons on the porch, in the shade between Paul's fields and the empty rooms that don't belong to me, don't belong to anyone. Outside, the distant twitter of two birds, nothing more.

This day returns every summer. It's back with me now, as I write this, trying to ignore the city — the wordless noise of cars, the worldless world's cries. On this day I am seventeen and getting lost, lost as though I'll never find my way back home again; lost in love with Paul, who is twice my age. I'm falling with the same despair with which I might fall off a cliff after a single misstep, tumbling eternally down. I don't say a word about it, not a word to anyone. These are secrets — the delight, the mismatch, the hopelessness. These are secrets everybody knows but me, I think. Paul knows, today, long before I find out, that days like this don't last. He knows that nothing lasts.

A pair of hummingbirds appears every day, outside one of the bedrooms no one uses, the one with nothing in it but a bed broken in two as though by an ax. The birds climb and dive around the eaves, slipping through the tracery of cherry trees. Every day I watch them spiral together in a double helix, in a spring dance. I watch the gnats bouncing and the spiders running; I can follow their tiny shadows in the grass. A faint rustle slowly fills the air, so slowly it takes me a long time to notice — a flutter in the world's roots.

All day long I speak to no one but the occasional caller, who only wants Paul. Many people want Paul, and sometimes he goes off at night with an apologetic smile, goes off to the rest of his life. "You can stay here if you want," he has said to me more than once, but I leave. Shook awake, I only mumble, No.

But this is truly summer. Paul is planting summer wheat, and winter dreams are laid bare and clean in wet shadows, to sprout along the earth's long curving beam. A veil stirs with the breeze of the day's ordered passage — and behind it, shapes I can't make out. My mouth is dusty from the field dirt that drifts in the air and settles on every surface, all over my skin.

The sink still holds the morning dishes, dripping with maple syrup. The sun falls across the floor, I am watching the water splash in the sink, and the silence is gone. I hear murmurs in the damp earth below. The breeze is turning to wind and it fills with sighs and soughing words too low to understand, the whisper of fruit ripened past its glory, tearing the skin, adding to the world's insistent roar. I stand in the kitchen alone, holding the glass, shot with light.

The day wears on. I watch Paul. There is a rope tied between my waist and Paul's; I feel the tug when he bends and lifts, I feel the pull when he walks away. He crosses the field to the far end, to that big stump he puzzles over, into the sun and dust. In the long grass the spiders capture flies and spin them tight, for later. The hummingbirds stroke the flowers with beaks as long and fine as a surgeon's lance.

In the field Paul is too far away to hear me if I cried, if I cried out, if I needed him. If we fell out of luck, into shadow, tomorrow, today, we would fall alone. The solid earth is as dizzy with dancing as the sea, moving me on past the farm and Paul, moving Paul past me. Even then, Paul was sick, and I didn't know.

The mere thought. The glimpse of so much loss is all it takes; it rakes across us like a knife, raises the truth up loud. The mere thought makes us, finally, more than willing to speak, to tell, tell the truth, our truth, every secret we know — to admit that flesh is meat and meat is flesh and the world spins on. Luck separates. No one gives it up without a fight.

The porch stays shaded all afternoon, the line between bright and dark. Below, dimness — below, where the roots are, sweat falls and blood falls and luck falls away, below, days end. Over and over, the world is made whole from its broken parts, over and over my hand holds the cold wet glass, Paul plants in the field, and the earth fills with singing all night long; all this without end, winter and summer, day and night, all this beneath the earth's curving beam, the water right beside me, the world's weary head in my lap. Love itself is what breaks our hearts; we fall into its rushing waters and tumble away, knocked breathless, cloven in two.

And the day goes finally by. A cradle rocking, rocking to stillness. I sit in my chair watching shadows growing tall and dark, like young sons coming forth. Our friend David drives straight to the steps in his dirty white convertible. David comes to visit almost every day; this week, he and Paul are fixing a truck. He grabs a toolbox and climbs over the windshield and the hood of the car and right over the porch rail, to stand beside me. He is big and bare-chested and never seems tired.

I look at David again, quiet beside me with a toolbox in his hand, and I see the rough gray along his temples, the slight sag along his neck, and realize with a start that David is old. David is beneath the earth's curving beam with all the rest of us, a body, a shadow, dying. "What's wrong?" he asks, and I shake my head, and he looks at my strange face, and the world spins to summer with a gasp of gratitude.

We talk about the wheat going in tomorrow. We talk about the little maple tree, still alive. We don't talk about how our lives are fettered one to the other in the perfumed soil of the spring. Then, I didn't know even that much.

A few years after today, the century-old farmhouse is taken apart. It's not in Paul's hands; he tries to stop the ruin and he cannot. Dozens of people come to help him one summer afternoon, to save what can be saved, to salvage what remains. And when the siding of the big bedroom where we used to sleep is removed, Paul finds an antique cache, a child's secret treasure — a book, a comb, a tiny tin generations old. "Here," he says, giving me the tin, "you keep this," and we go back to work. And a few years later, Paul dies, seeing it coming, almost ready. I wish I could tell him what I've learned since then; that grieving is a lifelong gift, that grieving is our one chance to cherish another without reservation.

But that was later. For now, today, Paul is coming home. I can see him getting closer, step by step, coming back to me, twenty years ago. Another car turns the corner too fast and feels the pull, taking the curve of the world too sudden and fast. Paul stops to watch the car go by. After awhile David goes into the dark house and turns the radio to another station, and then it plays only cool jazz in the darkening sky.

Secret Languages

Secret writing and codes are one thing, secret spoken languages another. Numerous special languages have been devised to disguise conversations or otherwise hide them from unwanted listeners. Some are so simple and well known as to hardly be secret at all; others are complex and private.

Many children and grandchildren of immigrants, having not learned the language of the homeland, have found themselves excluded by the use of the native tongue — suddenly a secret language.

Most of us, as children, learned Pig Latin in the schoolyard. But there are lots of similar inventions, some with even sillier names, for example, Boontling, Kinyume, and Iggity. They often rely on adding or switching certain types of sounds, syllables, or words according to a set of rules.

Lovers and thieves have long used secret languages, often of their own invention, to hide their activities.

And we've probably all experienced the exclusion of listening to a group of people from a particular profession speak to one another in its jargon.

The secrecy of language can be transparent or deeply hidden, intentional or not, even in everyday conversations.

Secrets: Who Doesn't Know?

Marvin Bell

"My life, my secret," wrote the poet James Wright.

Our friend Barbara is known as Bobbie the Artist by the circus with which she travels part of each year. Dorothy and I drive to a nearby town to hang around the back lot, see the show, and watch them tear down afterwards. We don't know where the circus has set up but we know how to find it. Once we take the exit from the Interstate, we look for arrows attached to the poles of road signs. Arrows up mean straight ahead. Arrows pointed down mean that a turn is coming. Each circus has its own arrow design, and the arrows are left behind when the troupe moves on: hence, one circus is said to have followed a previous year's arrows to the wrong lot. It isn't exactly secret knowledge that the way is marked by arrows, but generally people don't know. The circus has many other secrets — secrets of the midway, performing secrets of the big top. Among circus workers, last names and home towns go unsaid in case someone doesn't want to be found.

A secret is defined by those who are not supposed to know. Who can say that secrets are good or bad? The good and bad overlap. There are military secrets that must be kept for a campaign to succeed, but what about military secrets that, if revealed, would prevent needless bloodshed? Do you remember "The Pentagon Papers?" What happened at Ruby Ridge and for what reason?

There are lies taken for truth because they are leaked as if they were secrets. Newspapers live by taking things out of context so that much of the daily newspaper now seems to be information on the edge of secrecy. Organized from the top down, newspapers increasingly exist to sell advertising, and sales accrue to those that titillate and shock. Such is the character of a marketplace ethic, which, beholden to the bottom line in a dog-eat-dog global economy, and seeing a populace imprisoned by fear of the future, rarely factors in the good of anyone else. People have to make a living, and they will do it, if necessary, at the expense of others. Secrets are the natural outgrowth of competition.

And of oppression — political or social. In Yugoslavia in 1983, a group of us were taking an evening walk around the lake in Bled, Slovenia, during a PEN conference. The fellow walking next to me walked slower and slower until the rest of the group were well ahead. Then he spoke to me again of an ongoing issue: whether it would be safe to bring me to a protest meeting in Belgrade concerning the imprisonment of a certain poet for a line in his book of poems. As always, we had to speak privately — in secret.

Eastern Europe was once *the* place to study sophisticated secrecy. I had already had some experience in the encoded talk of Eastern Europe, still then under the overt domination of the Soviet Republic. At a banquet celebrating the end of a literary festival in Sarajevo the week before, a town official spoke to me during dinner of the greatness of the United States, first with reference to World War II and then to the presidency. He carefully praised the presidency, but never the President. The *Presidency* of the United States, he assessed more than once, is worthy of respect. Translation: your current President is a dope.

Later that evening, I went with my translator to a young poets' bar. Speaking in Serbo-Croatian, she explained that I was an American poet. One of the young writers lifted his glass and said (in English), "Fuck Reagan!" Then he asked if I were a Republican or a

Democrat. "Neither," I said, through my translator. "Independent."
"Ah," he said, raising his glass in toast, "Anarchista!"

It occurs to me that a true anarchism might permit no secrets.
Except for a society in which every person makes every decision first
in terms of the welfare of others, I can't conceive of a society without secrets. (And I haven't even touched on the kind of secret which
is kept expressly for the sake of others.)

In the meantime, we are left to consider whether everyone needs,
wishes or *can* know everything about anything. We are left with the
problem of separating what is news from what is journalism and deciding among truths. The study of ethics feeds off such ambivalent
scenarios. You know a secret that, if divulged, will help one person
but hurt two others. Or your child has a great time waiting for
Christmas but keeps asking if there's a Santa. And at the bridge tournament, you pick up a hand that is unshuffled and thus still ar-
ranged by suit, after which the bid is three passes to you. You now
realize that the hand was passed out and that you can make a bid of
"one no-trump." It is against the rules to employ such knowledge.
You can call over the tournament director and have the hand thrown
out, thus distorting the evening's play for everyone; shuffle your
hand and pass, thus passing up a chance for you and your partner to
score big; or bid one no-trump for the chance of gaining a "top
board" score for that hand. Such a minor secret, such a tiny decision, so easy to bite the bullet and pass, thus puffing up your sense
of integrity. But of such dilemmas are made the scenarios of much
weightier issues. Few social or political decisions afford the luxury
of deciding between good and bad. Instead, the possibilities range
from the "best best" through the "worst worst."

We don't like to think this, but even the worst acts of dictators
have been kept secret because, while they were bad for some people
they were good for them. A secret is a seesaw with victims on one
end and benefactors on the other. Sometimes it is unclear as to who
should sit where: the victim is part benefactor and vice-versa.

In the meantime we go on thinking that secrets are either thrilling (the covert, the arcane, the cryptic), money-in-our-pockets

(beauty secrets, recipes), or potentially destructive (dirty secrets, family skeletons). In fact, many secrets are a form of denial, often necessary, sometimes frivolous. What does it imply that a deodorant for women is named "Secret?" Is it a secret that women perspire? Is it private knowledge that women, too, have bodily functions? Gosh. Blame the idiots who decided to work the idea that women must appear to be something they are not.

It's a secret where the head of the corporation lives. How to reach the CEO who just "downsized" fifteen hundred people out of their jobs is a company secret. It's confidential. It's need-to-know, and your lost salary isn't need enough. The reason it's a secret is that institutions need to stay in the shadows. Secrets are the darkness in which slugs thrive. Oliver North had a basement office.

Did you have a magic decoder ring? Secrets are thrilling when you are first let in on them. Later you find out that you were told in order to make you a partner in crime.

Is it a secret that things end? Only grownups know, so is it a secret? Is it a secret that we live well at the expense of others? In other words, is the nature of the human condition a secret? Will the truth about anything less comprehensive than, say, death or *The Tao*, truly set you free?

Should the doctor tell the patient right off that he is dying? Should the cancer patient tell others, knowing that people will begin to keep her at arm's length or that she will be unable thereafter to escape the subject in conversation? Does the victim of a crime always help himself by coming forward? Is your sexual life to be announced publicly because someone else suffers the effect of your privacy?

What do I feel like inside? Who am I, really? Can we meet this side of fear? Dare we? We would like to believe that true friendship will survive any revelation, but the evidence suggests otherwise. We learn as we go.

"My life, my secret." Too complex to take credit or blame. Impossible to explain. Unworkable to hold in contempt any part of what it means to be a human being. There are awful secrets out there. Beyond instances of physical abuse and deprivation, we dare not pull out another's secret. On the level of emotions, we live at a distance from one another. Still, there are ways — sex and long intimacy, for example — in which we sometimes cross most of that distance, but never all of it. We die alone. How totally wonderful, therefore, that we live near others. If it is good to know oneself, it is twice good to know oneself in the presence of another.

Bios

Dorothy Allison is the author of *Bastard Out of Carolina* (1992 National Book Award Finalist in Fiction), *Trash* (1989 double Lambda Literary Award winner for Lesbian Fiction and Small Press Book), and *The Women Who Hate Me*, (Poetry, 1980-1990). "A Question of Class" is from her latest book, a collection of essays titled *Skin: Talking About Sex, Class & Literature* (1994).

Beth Bailey is a graphic designer in Rochester, New York. Her poetry has appeared in *Poetry Motel, Limestone, Sonoma Mandela* and *Gerbil — a queer culture zine.* She was one of thirteen poets to have work included in a national art/poetry show, "Imagination," in Suffolk, Long Island in 1993. "My biggest secret is that one of my brothers almost became a gay adolescent suicide statistic because he didn't think he could talk with anyone about his feelings. I dedicate the publication of this poem to him and hope that someday gay teens won't be made to feel as he did."

Marvin Bell is the author of thirteen books, the latest of which are *The Book of the Dead Man* (poems) and *A Marvin Bell Reader* (selected poems and prose). He is currently the Flannery O'Connor Professor of Letters at the University of Iowa's Writers' Workshop, and also lives in Port Townsend, Washington. His poetry appeared in Left Bank, *Pursuit of Happiness.* Marvin notes that in 1995 he celebrated his fifteenth consecutive year of not running the Honolulu Marathon.

Hollis Giammatteo lives in the San Juan Islands in Washington state where she has been hard at work in the uncovering of and healing from secrets. Her articles have been published in such magazines as *Ms., Women's Sports and Fitness, Vogue,* and the literary journals: *The North American Review, Prairie Schooner, Calyx,* and *Left Bank,* among others. She received a National Endowment for the Arts Literary Fellowship (1993) in support of *The People of Good Bye* (a novel in progress), and PEN/Jerard Fund Award for *On The Line: Memoir of a Peace Walk* (1988).

Dennis Held is a poet and editor who teaches at Lewis-Clark State College in Lewiston, Idaho. He won the University of Idaho's Wilderness Writing Award in 1994 for an essay that had nothing to do with wilderness. He once landed a poem in a major American magazine by writing a bogus cover letter in which he thanked the editor for his kind comments on his last group of poems — even though he had never sent the editor poems before. He never wanted to be an astronaut, and he loves to eat liver and onions at greasy spoons.

Cherie Hiser has photographed American subcultures for thirty years. The body of work is titled "The Odyssey of the Invisible" and includes "The Queens of Santa Fe," (1973–74) a group of culturally diverse gay men in New Mexico; "One of a Kind," (1974–79) hospitalized mental patients in Portland; and "Letters to Pepper," (1979–present) people who have tattoo work by artist Don Nolan of St. Paul, Minnesota. She is currently working on "Re:Visions," a series on aging: portraits of the same people taken twenty-five years apart. She is collaborating with Portland writer Sandra Stone on a portrait/narrative suite titled "Sleight of Face." Cherie is a third generation Portlander and teaches photography nationwide.

Keri Hulme: *The Silences Between: Maoriki Conversations*, poetry, Oxford University Press, Auckland; *The Bone People*, a novel (Spiral), won The Booker award; *Lost Possessions*, a poetry/prose play (Victoria University Press); *Kaihau: The Wind Eater*, short stories (Victoria University Press); *Home Places*, "essays and poems about the places I love particularly," in collaboration with photographer Robin Morrison (Hodder and Stoughton); *Strands*, poetry; *Bait*, a novel forthcoming from Viking Penguin in the United States, Macmillan in New Zealand, and Picador in England.

Elizabeth Hurst was born in Los Angeles and has lived in San Francisco for many years. She began writing poetry in the early eighties. Secret: "I watch the Home Shopping Channel."

Toni Kennedy, a native Oregonian, began to write about her life as a nun when people wanted those secrets more than her children's stories or novel.

"Once I left the convent, I planned to bury my past in the desert. After ten years I unearthed the memories and found replicas at home. I still pray, hike left of center, and teach adolescents. Now that I'm writing this book of essays, I realize the cloister will always be with me. I don't mind as much anymore. It's fun to be fifty plus and able to slip through the Needle's Eye."

Charles Ostman is science editor for *Mondo 2000*, and technical editor for *Midnight Engineering* magazine, a national trade journal for the entrepreneurial engineering community. He has been involved with recent developments in nanotechnology, including the creation of models of virtual nano-environments, molecular assembly components and component systems, self replicating and self modifying molecular "machines," quasi-viral components and pseudo-organelles, and other related areas of nanotechnology. Charles began his career with eight years at Lawrence Berkeley Laboratory, and other sites in the national laboratory system, which included work on the early development of shape changing alloys and their applications. This was followed by 14 years of work at the microwave systems development lab at GTE Lenkurt, optical recognition and machine vision related hardware development at Integrated Automation (division of Litton Industries), electronic hardware design at the DroidWorks (then a division at Lucas Films), and a variety of independently supported technical development projects.

Tamar Perla's short stories have been published in the magazine *Ascent*, a local zine *Frighten the Horses*, *Erotic Fiction Quarterly*, and most recently in *Literal Latte*, a Manhattan coffeehouse journal. Last spring she completed her graduate degree in creative writing at San Francisco State University and is currently working on a collection of short stories.

Rick Rubin returned neither to Brooklyn nor to social work after his brief career on Bushwick Ave. where he served a tour of duty as infantryman in President Lyndon Baines Johnson's War on Poverty. The war lost, he retreated to prepared positions in what was later to become trendified, materialistic Northwest Portland, Oregon. Still there, he continues to observe the caperings of the beautiful people with wry amazement. Northwest was as shirt-sleeve a neighborhood as you could imagine while he was growing up there. Everything changes, yet, even gentrified to the glitz, Northwest Portland beats Williamsburg Brooklyn all hollow in the easy living department.

Sallie Tisdale is the author of several books, including *Talk Dirty to Me*, and is a contributing editor at *Harper's*. She has many secrets but isn't very good at keeping them.

Nance Van Winckel's first collection of short stories, *Limited Lifetime Warranty*, appeared in 1994 with University of Missouri Press. *The Dirt*, her second collection of poems, is recently out from Miami University Press. Nance directs the creative writing program at Eastern Washington University, where she edits *Willow Springs*. Secret: "I was a member, for two hours in 1971, of the SDS (Students for a Democratic Society). They didn't like it that I brought my knitting to the meeting and told me I wouldn't be welcome back."

David Xiao was born in Hong Kong, lived in Taiwan, New York, and Minneapolis, and currently resides in Seattle. He received an M.F.A. from the University of Washington, is now a part-time creative writing instructor there, and recently received a fellowship from Artist Trust of Seattle. David is working on a novel, a love story set in central China during the early months of the Cultural Revolution. He is also working on a book of short stories revolving around the theme of "home." He and his wife, Joyce, recently had their first child in September. Secret: "Well…I once failed the Pepsi Challenge."

Lidia Yuknavitch is the editor of *two girls review*, a recent Ph.D. (pronounced "fud"), and a writer. Her stories have appeared in *The Northwest Review, Quarry West, Puerto del Sol, The Rain City Review, Postmodern Culture,* and *The Cream City Review*. She loves words, images, panties in the freezer, and dogs. She is blonde, bi, in love, impolite, and fierce.

Matt Yurdana has an M.F.A. from the University of Montana, where he also received the Richard Hugo Memorial Scholarship and the Academy of American Poets Award. His poems have appeared in *CutBank, Talking River Review*, and *Poetry Northwest*. Secret: "Throughout my childhood I was terrified of flies."

Code of the Road

The following signs, many placed throughout the book, have long been used by hobos as a means of helping those who follow. They are only a few of the many, but they give a flavor of this secret language.

AFRAID

DISHONEST
(UNDEPENDABLE)

HERE

ALL RIGHT

DOG

BAD DOG

DON'T GIVE UP

IF SICK, WILL GIVE
CARE

BE GOOD (RELIGIOUS)

DOUBTFUL

IN

GENTLEMAN

JAIL

BE PREPARED TO
DEFEND YOURSELF

GO

DANGER

HALT

JUDGE

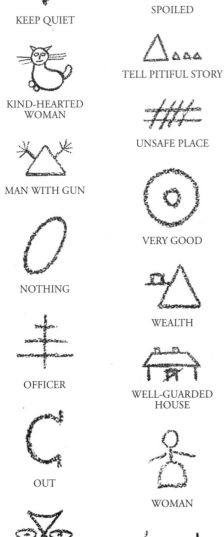

KEEP QUIET

SPOILED

YOU WILL BE BEATEN

KIND-HEARTED
WOMAN

TELL PITIFUL STORY

MAN WITH GUN

UNSAFE PLACE

NOTHING

VERY GOOD

OFFICER

WEALTH

OUT

WELL-GUARDED
HOUSE

SAFE CAMP

WOMAN

YOU MAY CAMP HERE

LEFT BANK BOOKS

A GREAT WAY TO READ BETWEEN THE LINES

BORDER & BOUNDARIES — Flee with the Bedouins, secede from the Union, travel with Michael Dorris, Diana Abu-Jaber, William Stafford, Sandra Scofield, Larry Colton. #5. ISBN 0-936085-58-4; ~~$9.95~~. ONLY $5!

EXTINCTION — Get it before it's gone. David Suzuki introduces Sallie Tisdale, Tess Gallagher, Barry Lopez, Nancy Lord, David Quammen, Robert Michael Pyle, John Callahan, and others, as they look at the disappearance and rebirth of languages, lakes, poetry, and cultures. #2. ISBN 0-936085-50-9; ~~$7.95~~. ONLY $4!

GOTTA EARN A LIVING — Know them by their work: two baker's dozen, including Norman Maclean, Kate Braid, Gary Snyder, David James Duncan, Teri Zipf, Sherman Alexie, Sibyl James, and Robin Cody. #4. ISBN 0-936085-54-1; ~~$7.95~~. ONLY $4!

HEAD/WATERS — Brenda Peterson swims with dolphins, Marc Reisner *(Cadillac Desert)* consorts with rice barons, David James Duncan *(Brothers K)* imagines himself a salmon, Gary Snyder becomes the river, Pam Houston *(Cowboys Are My Weakness)* falls for whitewater, and more on baptisms, bathings, drownings. ISBN 0-936085-28-2; ~~$9.95~~. ONLY $5!

KIDS' STUFF — Judge a society by the way it treats its children. Take a look at the world of kids through the eyes of Mikal Gilmore, Sallie Tisdale, Sherman Alexie, Ann Rule, Virginia Euwer Wolff, Shani Mootoo, and others. Definitely not for kids. #6. ISBN 0-936085-26-6; ~~$9.95~~. ONLY $5!

PURSUIT OF HAPPINESS — How do we interpret that enigmatic phrase in the Declaration of Independence? John Nichols *(Milagro Beanfield War)*, Marvin Bell *(The Book of the Dead Man)*, Craig Lesley *(The Sky Fisherman)*, Lynda Sexson *(Margaret of the Imperfections)*, and others pursue their visions, or are pursued by them. ISBN 0-936085-30-4; ~~$11.95~~. ONLY $6!

SEX, FAMILY, TRIBE — Get intimate with Ursula Le Guin, William Stafford, Ken Kesey, Colleen McElroy, Matt Groening, William Kittredge, Charles Johnson, and many more. #3. ISBN 0-936085-53-5; ~~$7.95~~. ONLY $4!

WRITING & FISHING THE NORTHWEST — Consider the cast. Wallace Stegner, Greg Bear, Craig Lesley, Sharon Doubiago, Nancy Lord, John Keeble. #1. ISBN 0-936085-19-3; ~~$7.95~~. ONLY $4!

INDIVIDUALS, PHOTOCOPY THE ORDER FORM ON THE LAST PAGE, OR ASK FOR LEFT BANK BOOKS AT YOUR FAVORITE BOOKSTORE. BOOKSTORES, CONTACT US FOR ORDERING INFORMATION.

LEFT BANK BOOKS
GREAT WRITING. GREAT READING.
AND A GREAT HALF-PRICE SPECIAL.
ORDER NOW AND SAVE!

For yourself or any thoughtful friend.

Just copy this page, fill in the form below, and send it today. Other titles are available (see previous page); add $3 shipping for the first book and $1 for each additional book.

Send the Left Bank Books noted below to me at:

Send the gift books noted below to:

I'd like the following editions (indicate if gift):

My order total is:

I've enclosed a check ☐ or Money Order ☐ — or charge my VISA ☐ or MC ☐; its number and expiration are:

VISA/MC orders may be placed at 503.621.3911, faxed to 503.621.9826, emailed to bhp@teleport.com, or mailed to Blue Heron Publishing, 24450 NW Hansen Road, Hillsboro, OR 97124.